The
Contemporary Monologue
Men

Edited with notes and commentaries by
MICHAEL EARLEY
& PHILIPPA KEIL

Methuen Drama

First published in Great Britain 1995
by Methuen Drama
an imprint of Reed Books Ltd
Michelin House, 81 Fulham Road, London SW3 6RB
and Auckland, Melbourne, Singapore and Toronto

Copyright in the selections, format, introductions and commentaries
© 1995 Michael Earley and Philippa Keil

The editors have asserted their moral rights

ISBN 0-413-68120-3

A CIP catalogue record for this book
is available at the British Library

Typeset by Wilmaset Ltd, Birkenhead, Wirral
Printed in Great Britain by Cox & Wyman Ltd, Reading, Berkshire

Front cover: Alan Rickman
Photograph by Ivan Kyncl

The Contemporary Monologue
Men

Michael Earley is Chief Producer of Plays for BBC Radio Drama in London. He was Chairman of the Theatre Studies Program at Yale University and taught acting, dramatic literature and playwriting there and at New York University's Tisch School of the Arts, The Juilliard School's Acting Program, Smith College and various other schools and universities in America and Britain.

Philippa Keil is a writer, editor and translator who trained at the Yale School of Drama. She graduated from Sussex University where she acted, directed and produced plays for the Frontdoor Theatre, and then worked professionally in London at Richmond's Orange Tree Theatre.

by the same authors

The Contemporary Monologue (Women)
The Modern Monologue (Men and Women)
The Classical Monologue (Men and Women)
Soliloquy! The Shakespeare Monologues (Men and Women)
Solo: The Best Monologues of the 80s (Men and Women)

Contents

Notes to the Actor

The monologues in this volume come from plays produced and published in Britain and America over the past ten years. Each identifies some facet of contemporary thought and feeling. They augment the speeches in our two previous volumes, *The Modern Monologue* and *The Classical Monologue*, as well as supplement and update a volume we published a number of years ago, *Solo: The Best Monologues of the 80s*. Our aim in all these books has been to provide actors with the kind of material that holds the stage and challenges the performer to use skills that will show him to best advantage.

When we put these volumes together we deliberately choose speeches from plays that are in print and readily available. (See *Play Sources* at the end of this volume.) You simply must read the whole play for the fullest context of any speech. A monologue can never be the whole story of a particular drama. It is always just one character's point of view at an isolated moment in the action. One story linked to many others. As an actor, you cannot possibly glean all that is relevant about a character's life, likes and dislikes, behaviour, place in the plot or even why he speaks unless you have followed that character's progress through the entire play. You have to know the playwright's style and what he or she is attempting to say in these isolated moments and how to weigh it against other scenes and speeches. A collection of monologues like this can get an actor started but should take you back to the plays from which these speeches have been selected.

To help you begin your work on these pieces our Introductions summarize a play's action up to the point the speech begins. We have also tried to give you a brief sketch of the character that might be helpful, using where possible the playwright's own words. In the Commentary after each monologue we alert you to details in the speech that could help you to act it better. A warning though: *these are not director's notes*, since our aim is not to dictate how these monologues should be performed. That's a job we must leave open to each individual performer. But any good dramatist includes notes of direction in the very rhythm and structure of speeches and dialogue. So what we have done in each Commentary is to put you on the trail of these vital stylistic clues so you can appeciate what the writer has given you to act. In most instances the path of a speech is self-evident and needs little gleaning. But since we work with actors on a daily basis, we know that even the smallest observations and hints about the language of a speech can help improve a performance: the repetition of a single word, an obsession with a prop, the way a character seems to be avoiding something unspoken or the way he expresses a vital need are all the kinds of clues you can find in the character's choice of words.

What makes the monologues which follow so contemporary is their common currency and their ability to engage with life as we live it now. As contemporary events bear down on us playwrights respond to the crises and pressures in different ways. Practically all the speeches in this book are preoccupied with self-contradictions of one kind or another. Loneliness and sexual conflict, for example, are two themes which are repeated again and again. A character always speaks out in a play because he has something to say and must be heard. An actor has to listen to the character in order to really hear what he is saying. Perhaps the only and best bit of direction to leave you with when doing a monologue is to feel the need to speak, know what you are speaking about and to whom, and the words will connect with what you have to say.

Michael Earley
Philippa Keil
London 1995

Angels in America Part One:
Millennium Approaches
Tony Kushner

Act 3, scene 6. Roy's office, Manhattan. Late winter, 1985–86.

Roy M. Cohn (40s–50s) is 'a successful New York lawyer and unofficial power broker. . . . Roy conducts business with great energy, impatience, and sensual abandon.' He is Jewish and right-wing. He is also homosexual and has contracted AIDS, but he keeps this a secret to protect his positon: '. . . what I am is defined entirely by who I am. Roy Cohn is not a homosexual. Roy Cohn is a heterosexual man . . . who fucks around with guys . . . AIDS is what homosexuals have. I have liver cancer.' Despite having access to the White House, he is an outsider and a loner excluded from the very circles he scorns yet yearns to join. The pursuit of power and money is his greatest love: he is cynical and dismissive of all other kinds of love and human relationships. People are not individuals, merely pawns in the power games he plays. During the 1950s he was the right-hand man to his mentor, Senator Joe McCarthy who masterminded the Communist witch-hunts. Cohn is 'unorthodox' and criminal in his legal and business dealings and the American Bar Association is trying to ban him from practice. He is trying to get a young lawyer, Joe, to take up a position in the Justice Department where he would be able to 'exert influence' on the hearings. In this scene Joe finally declines to take up the position in Washington because of resistance from his wife Harper and Roy explodes with typical vehemence. He is by now a very sick man and his last hope of professional redemption has just been denied him.

ROY. You're not dead, boy, you're a sissy. You love me; that's moving, I'm moved. It's nice to be loved. I warned you about her, didn't I, Joe? But you don't listen to me, why, because you say Roy is smart and Roy's a friend but

I

Roy . . . well, he isn't nice, and you wanna be nice. Right? A nice, nice man! (*Little pause.*) You know what my greatest accomplishment was, Joe, in my life, what I am able to look back on and be proudest of? And I have helped make Presidents and unmake them and mayors and more goddam judges than anyone in NYC ever – AND several million dollars, tax-free – and what do you think means the most to me? You ever hear of Ethel Rosenberg? Huh, Joe, huh?
[JOE. Well, yeah, I guess I . . . Yes.]
Yes. Yes. You have heard of Ethel Rosenberg. Yes. Maybe you even read about her in the history books. If it wasn't for me, Joe, Ethel Rosenberg would be alive today, writing some personal advice column for *Ms.* magazine. She isn't. Because during the trial, Joe, I was on the phone every day, talking with the judge . . .
[JOE. Roy . . .]
Every day, doing what I do best, talking on the telephone, making sure that timid Yid nebbish on the bench did his duty to America, to history. That sweet unprepossessing woman, two kids, boo-hoo-hoo, reminded us all of our little Jewish mamas – she came this close to getting life; I pleaded till I wept to put her in the chair. Me. I did that. I would have fucking pulled the switch if they'd have let me. Why? Because I fucking hate traitors. Because I fucking hate communists. Was it legal? Fuck legal. Am I a nice man? Fuck nice. They say terrible things about me in *The Nation*. Fuck *The Nation*. You want to be Nice, or you want to be Effective? Make the law, or be subject to it. Choose. Your wife chose. A week from today, she'll be back. SHE knows how to get what SHE wants. Maybe I ought to send *her* to Washington.

COMMENTARY: At a late moment in the play, in the midst of an argument with a young protégé – and potential lover – Roy Cohn explodes in anger. Throughout Kushner's play tensions, like the spreading disease AIDS, mount only to overflow in eruptions like this. Cohn reveals a recurring preoccupation which both made his career and branded him forever as someone infamous: the executions of Julius and Ethel Rosenburg. Interestingly, he singles out only Ethel Rosenburg in this diatribe. Someone who 'reminded us all of our little Jewish mamas'. She will appear to him at crucial moments in the play just as Richard III's dead victims appear to him in the last act of Shakespeare's tragedy. There is nothing soft about Roy Cohn. In fact, an actor playing him has to search hard to find positive values in the character. His overwhelming sense of pride, power and influence are certainly rich facets of the character which can be brought out in the open. This is a man who will stop at nothing to get what he wants. He argues forcefully and, as a lawyer, is used to putting his case across with colourful emphasis.

Assassins
Stephen Sondheim (music and lyrics) and
John Weidman (book)

Scene 14. A highway outside Washington D.C., February 1974.

Sam Byck (44) is divorced and unemployed. He has few, if any, friends. He becomes obsessed with sending long, rambling tape recordings to a number of celebrities with whom he feels a special connection; including the composer and conductor Leonard Bernstein. He is also convinced that the American political system is fundamentally corrupt and he donates what little money he has to organizations like the Black Liberation Army. On Christmas Eve 1973 he picketed the White House dressed in a Santa Claus suit. He dreams up a plan, which he calls 'Pandora's Box', to assassinate President Richard Nixon. He plans to hijack a commercial jet, crashing it into the White House. In this scene he is in his car en route to the airport. As he drives he talks into a portable tape recorder.

Lights up on Sam Byck, behind the wheel of a '67 Buick, driving down a highway late at night. He looks bleary-eyed and strung out. The jacket of his Santa suit is unbuttoned, revealing a dirty T-shirt and a greasy set of suspenders. On the seat beside him are his tape recorder, a jumble of tapes, his Santa Claus beard, a copy of the Baltimore Sun, *a couple of cans of Budweiser and a paper bag from Burger King. He reaches into the Burger King bag, pulls out a hamburger and takes a bite* . . .

BYCK. 'Have It Your Way.' You know what my way is? *Hot.* How 'bout a hamburger that's fucking hot?! (*He hurls the hamburger out the window. A car horn blares.*) Don't blame me! I'm from Massachusetts! (*He laughs, digs in the bag, pulls out a fistful of French fries, and talks into the tape recorder.*)

4

Dick, you still there, babe? Sorry about that. Ten miles from the airport, I'm starting to lose it here. Stay with me, baby. Talk me down – ! (*He shoves the French fries in his mouth and takes a long drink of beer*.) You know, Dick, in this, the waning hours of your administration, it seems appropriate to look back at your long years of public service and to conclude that, as our President, you really bit the big one. Wazoo city, babe. What can I say? And you know what? This cracks me up. I voted for you! Yes! I gave you my vote, my sacred democratic trust, and you know what you did? You pissed all over it! . . . Well, what the hell. Guys like you, you piss all over everything. You piss all over the country. You piss all over yourselves. You piss all over me . . . Yeah, yeah, I know. 'Sam, don't say it! You're my main man! Guys like you, you're the backbone of the nation! Sammy – ' (*Exploding*.) *Shut up, Dick! I'm* talking now, all right?! I'm talking and *you're* listening! Here – (*He slaps the newspaper*.) You seen a paper lately?! 'Grandma Lives In Packing Crate!' 'Sewage Closes Jersey Beaches!' 'Saudi Prince Buys Howard Johnson's!' What the hell is going on here, Dick?! It wasn't supposed to be like this. It wasn't but it *is*. And schmucks like you, you're telling us it *isn't*! Everything is fine! It's great! It's *Miller Time*! *What* Miller Time?! The woods are burning, Dick! What can we do?! We want to make things *better*! *How*?! Let's hold an election! *Great*. The Democrat says he'll fix everything, the Republicans fucked up. The Republican says he'll fix everything, the Democrats fucked up. Who's telling us the truth? Who's lying? *Someone's* lying. *Who*? We read, we guess, we argue, but deep down we know that we don't know. How can we? Oil embargoes, megatons, holes in the ozone. Who can understand this crap? We need to believe, to trust like little kids, that someone wants what's best for us, that someone's looking out for us. That someone loves us. Do they? *No*. They lie to us! They lie about what's right, they lie about

5

what's wrong, they lie about the fuckin' hamburgers! And when we realize they're lying, really realize it in our gut, then we get scared. Then we get terrified. Like children waking in the dark, we don't know where we are. 'I had a bad dream! Mommy! Daddy! Sammy had a nightmare!' And daddy comes and takes me in his arms and says, 'It's O.K., Sammy. Daddy's here. I love you, kid. Your mommy doesn't, but I do.' And mommy comes and holds me tight and says, 'I've got you, Bubala. I'm here for you. Your daddy isn't, but I am.' . . . And then where are we? Who do we believe? What do we do?! (*A beat.*) We do what we have to do. We kill the President.

COMMENTARY: Sam is on the way to commit an assassination. A divided character, he's full of both fear *and* bravado. Throughout the speech the tension grows. Every gesture and word from Sam (his shouts out the window, the way he stabs into the packet of fries) illustrate this mounting tension. Sam is both urging himself on towards his goal and trying to find reasons to pull back. ('Stay with me, baby. Talk me down – !': the words of a suicide). He's both pushed and pulled as he speaks. His head is also full of disconnected dialogue and masses of confusion. He sees himself as President Nixon's equal. But he's isolated and alone, terrified of the dark like a child, 'bleary-eyed and strung out'. Embedded in the monologue are enough details for you to know that Sam may have been abandoned as a child. The final image of the child divided between mother and father, never wholly integrated and complete, is a major discovery for the actor. Following fast is the illogical decision to 'kill the President'. This is the decisive moment the speech has been building towards.

Babies
Jonathan Harvey

Act 2, scene 4. Viv Williams's bedroom in a house on a Thames-mead housing estate in South London. 1994.

Joe (24) is a Learning Support teacher and a tutor of form 9CY at a south east London Comprehensive School. He is originally from Liverpool and 'he speaks with a broad Liverpool twang'. He is very popular with his rowdy and often difficult students but he has kept the fact that he is gay well hidden from them. He lives with his lover, Woody, an electrician, but Woody's dependence on drugs angers Joe. When Joe is invited to a birthday party for Tammy, one of his students, he rashly accepts but he leaves Woody at home. As the party progresses and everyone gets more and more drunk, Joe has to fend off sexual advances from both Tammy's mother Viv and her homosexual uncle, Kenny. In this scene Kenny has been chatting up and feeling up Joe. Joe tries to stall Kenny by revealing that he lives with someone and when Kenny asks if he loves Woody this is Joe's reply.

[KENNY. Good. (*Pause.*) D'you love him? (*Pause.*) What's he up to tonight then? (*Beat.*) Out boozin'? (*Pause.*) Pretend I'm a class o'kids, it might be easier to fucking talk then.]
JOE. I love him, but . . . he . . . he fucking kills me. (*Beat.*) D'you know how it feels? To stand in a street in broad daylight trying to sort your problems out? To stand outside a pub on a Sunday afternoon and . . . you're talking to him and you know he's off his face, and this big bastard comes up – straight as a die, but he knows he can make his money outa the queens – and he comes up and he says 'Here Woody' and he hands him a little slip o'paper, the tiniest slip o'paper with a little blue dot on it, and I feel that much of a lowy I

7

pay for it and the big bastard goes away. And then your fella stands there and rips it in two, sticks one bit in his pocket, and the other in his mouth . . . and keeps on talking . . . About us, and the way we are, and the way . . . I make him feel. 'You're hogging me Joe, I need me mates.' And I just wanna say, 'Can't you wait five minutes? Can't you just wait 'til I've gone and you're back with your mates? Can't you take your acid then?' (*Shakes his head*.) I used to like me, and the way I feel about me. But when you're with someone else it's like . . . it's . . . well it's like you've got a mirror on your shoulder, and what you see in them . . . is how you see yourself. Like it's reflected. And if they're being a twat to you . . . then . . . you think you're a twat yourself, you don't question it. You can't. (*Beat*.) Am I talking shite?

COMMENTARY: Joe and his lover Woody share a relationship that is out of synch. The speech uncovers the tension that lies between them. In this scene and an earlier one, Joe has been unable to articulate why he and Woody don't work as a couple. Each are rubbed the wrong way. They're incompatible though in love. Joe pays for Woody's drug habit. Notice how the speech takes a nosedive. The more Joe finds divisive examples the more the relationship falls apart in what we hear. His anxiety, hastened by his drunken state and Kenny's advances up his leg, make him less and less coherent.

Belfry
Billy Roche

Act 1. The belfry of a Roman Catholic church in Wexford, a small town in Ireland.

Artie O'Leary (40s) is the sacristan of the local church. He lives with his bed-ridden mother and his sheltered life revolves around the church. His father, according to his mother, was a 'Jack the lad' who callously abandoned them. Throughout Artie's childhood and adulthood the image of his absent father is a constant influence. He's a man whose life feels 'kind of small'; the complete opposite of his father. During the play Artie learns that this image of his father is a creation of his mother's bitter anger. His father is not the 'boyo' that he imagined, but an 'ordinary' man who fathered an illegitimate child and left to make his way in England, honourably inviting mother and son to join him there. Artie is friendly and good-hearted. He has a romantic streak though he has never had a girlfriend. His predictable and lonely life is thrown into complete chaos when he unexpectedly falls passionately in love with Angela, a married woman with children who cleans the church. Their affair, which is as much of the heart and mind as of the body, is conducted clandestinely in the church belfry. Artie opens the play with this speech which is delivered some years after the events in the play.

ARTIE (*to the audience*). I know what they think of me. I know well enough what they say about me behind my back. There he goes, Artie O'Leary the poor little sacristan with the candle grease on his sleeve, smellin' of incense as he opens the big heavy belfry door. They watch me standin' quietly in the shadows of the mortuary when they come to bury their dead and they see me goin' home to my little empty house in the rain every night to listen to the news. Lonely auld days and nights they're thinkin'. Dreary auld

9

mornings too. Snuffin' out candles and emptyin' poor boxes. Of course they've all probably forgotten by now that I once loved a woman. Another man's wife. She came into this queer auld whisperin' world of mine to change the flowers in the chapel and to look after the altar and although she's been gone out of here over a year now I swear to God her fragrance still lingers about the place – in the transept, near the shrine. Around the vestry and above in the belfry – her scent . . . where ever I go . . . It's thanks to her that I have a past worth talkin' about at all I suppose. Although I often curse her for it. There are days now when I find myself draggin' her memory behind me everywhere I go. I bless her too though. She tapped a hidden reservoir inside of me that I didn't even know was there. Because of her I now find myself ramblin' into snooker halls and back room card games where, surrounded by archin' eyebrows, I become my father's son again and argue the toss with anyone who cares to step on my corns. And I must confess that I get a certain manly satisfaction from the fact that I can hold my own with the so-called big drinkers and small time gamblers of the town. Oh yes, a hidden reservoir she tapped . . . But before we all get carried away here I think I'd better point out to yeh that I'm more a man in mournin' than a hawk in the night. Because yeh see I know now for sure that she will not be comin' back to me. And so I mourn. And I pine. And everytime I come up here the sound of this lonely bell tells me that I'm goin' to live a long, long time. The only consolation I have is that at least now I have a story to tell.

COMMENTARY: Artie's opening speech is full of crucial information. He tells us who he is, what he does, what people think about him and the secret the play will explore – an illicit love affair and how it changed Artie. The speech also sets the scene for all the retrospective events which will form the plot of *Belfry*. When we listen to Artie we instantly hear someone who speaks in measured and moving sentences that are touched with poetry. We get the impression he is a good, simple man. He sounds a bit as though he's delivering a sermon to a hushed congregation. The easy conversational rhythms of the speech must be obeyed. The dialect is provincial Irish though it needn't be delivered in this way. We learn in the speech that Artie is a prisoner in a small Irish town. He still carries within him a sense memory of Angela, her 'scent' which still lingers in the church. She also 'tapped a hidden reservoir inside' Artie. This is a critical piece of direction from playwright to actor. You know that the journey Artie takes is not away from Wexford but to a place deep inside himself. He is mourning for the lost opportunities of his life.

Berlin Bertie
Howard Brenton

Act 1, scene 1. Alice's ground-floor flat on a South London housing estate. Good Friday, April 13th, 1990.

Sandy (25) does various dodgy odd jobs while claiming social security benefits. His current 'job' is hustling pirated videos in the local street market. He brims with enthusiasm and optimistic energy for everything he does. Alice, his girlfriend of one month, is a middle class social worker. He doesn't have a place of his own so he divides his time between his mother's flat and Alice's. The playwright describes Alice's chaotic flat in detail: 'There are piles of discarded newspapers, many of them torn and screwed up. There are unwashed plates and broken crockery amongst them. There is an ironing board that is piled with bottles, cans and the remains of take-away meals. There are discarded and unwashed clothes. There are lamps on the floor, some without shades and with a mess of wires. It is impossible to walk across the floor without treading on something or having to kick something out of the way. There is a crack diagonally across the window. It has been clumsily repaired with brown sticky tape. There are no curtains. There is a television set . . . Alice is lying asleep on the floor. She is swathed in old blankets . . . Sandy rails at the sleeping Alice. He is dressing.'

SANDY. Some fucking sense o' responsibility . . . I mean I'm not saying get a grip on your life, not that crap, I'm not saying stop being such a fucking slag, nothing GIANT, I'm not saying be a GOOD PERSON all of a sudden, I'm not saying 'say yes' to changing your life inside out when the fucking Mormons come round the door, I'm not saying BE A SAINT, I'm just saying clear up the fucking Chinese takeaway. I'm not even saying clear up the last Chinese takeaway, I'm saying clear up the last Chinese takeaway but three. Or four would do. (ALICE *suddenly sits bolt upright. Her hair is unkempt. She is sleeping in a grey-white singlet. There are dark rings around her eyes. She is staring with her mouth open.* SANDY *stares back at her. A silence. Then she collapses back without a sound and turns over.*) I mean even my mum clears up a bit! Nothing extreme, washing windows and that, nothing WILD, ironing underpants and that, but not even my mum, fucking slag she is and all, not even my mum lets something what's dripped go mouldy on the fucking TV screen . . . there is something what's dripped and gone mouldy on the fucking TV screen, I mean what are you trying to do, make A POINT? I mean, you watch the TV news, all the fucking time, all channels, channel hopping, same news over and over, I mean what is it with you, do you like to see what's going on in the fucking world through a smear of stuck-on sweet 'n' sour pork? I mean you are driving me mad, do you know that? Right I've decided, say nothing, I'll clear up the fucking TV screen myself, right? (*He is lost at how to do so. He returns to the attack.*) And where WAS you last night anyway? Me stuck here, waiting . . . I even watched the FUCKING NEWS for you . . . some fucking super gun . . . going in and out of some fucking country or other, Greece, Israel, Iran . . . I tried to remember, but I don't know foreign places, they just don't stick, I just don't know 'em, in't nowhere on the map 'cept ENGLAND far as I'm concerned . . . And anyway fell asleep, didn't I . . . right . . . clear up the . . . Right how do I do that? (*He pauses.*) Need a little aerosol can of something to clean something, don't you, yeah, a can. (*He kicks at the mess. He stumbles. He pickes up some newspaper. He tears it, making a wad. He looks around again and picks up an open lager can. It is empty. Then he finds a can with beer still in it. He wets the wad of newspaper with the beer. He goes to wipe the television screen. But he notices the wires leading to the television and video machine. They are botched together with insulating tape. The tape hangs ragged at a join. He touches the join. He receives an electric shock. The wire sticks to his fingers for a second.*) Aaaaaaaargh! (*He crouches. He is shivering. He retches and –*)

COMMENTARY: Sandy literally explodes onto the stage with a stunning opening monologue. He's an angry young man who has a tantrum. This is one of those risky and gripping opening moments where the actor comes onstage and has to operate at peak energy. He's both physically and verbally threatening. Words spew out of him like one long retch. The target of his rage, Alice, reacts for only an instant and then turns away, summoning a new wave of invective from Sandy. There is an age difference between the characters and, as we later find, this is clearly a relationship that doesn't work. So Sandy's anger comes from a host of sources. He's a man who has never left home and has probably never ventured far beyond a specific neighbourhood. He could just as easily be yelling at his mother. Despite all his anger, Sandy is trying to get Alice to pull herself together.

Boy with Beer
Paul Boakye

Act 1. A flat in London.

Donovan (21) is a bisexual Afro-Caribbean. He left school when he was fifteen and now works driving a van for a building company. At the moment he is living with Susan, "cos she's going through a bad patch'. He seems to be fond of her and hopes to have a child with her. He likes going out drinking (he does not smoke because of a chest infection) and dancing; especially to raves. He is streetwise, arrogant and confident. He likes fooling around and at school he was always known as the class joker. He is a self-confessed flirt and manipulates people with his 'boyish charm'. At the Bluenote Club, Donovan takes a fancy to Karl, a poet and photographer from Ghana, and he gets one of his friends to act as a go-between to check out Karl and his companion. Karl ends up inviting Donovan round for dinner the next evening. In this scene Donovan and Karl have been warily getting to know one another, with Donovan doing most of the talking. In this speech Donovan gives a taste of his lifestyle.

DONOVAN. I flirt with everyone, man. It's packed, ennit. You have to flirt with them jus' to get 'em out've your way. Hardcore's brilliant. You're just dancing there. Everybody doing their own thing. Moving their arms about like this. Wild, man, wild. The girls are just tripping and wriggling their arms in fronta your face like inviting you for a fuck. Then there's the boys. I love white boys at Hardcore, man. They'll do anything for you. Share their joints . . . their E's . . . their girls . . . even give you a lift right back to your own front door. Man, I mean, them white boys are so fucking good – I just love 'em. Step on a black guy's toe, you could

15

be dead within seconds, step on a white geeza's foot, he'll want to buy you a drink. (KARL *laughs*.) No, serious! The other night, right, I was pushing through this crowd. Where was I? – can't remember – anyway, I was pushing through this crowd. Spilt beer all down this white guy's shirt. I mean all the beer, all over him. The guy turned round, smiled, 'Don't worry about a thing, mate, naw it's awright. It's wet enuf in 'ere as it is.' Big grin across his face like this. Brushed it off. Just carried on dancing. I couldn't believe it. I wouldn't a done that, would you? I woulda brushed it off, but I wouldn't a smiled about it. I woulda said, 'That's awright, mate, just make fucking sure you don't do it again, awright cunt!?'

――――――――――

Donovan and Karl end up in bed together but their attempted love making is aborted: Donovan wants instant gratification, Karl wants romance. After they get dressed and leave the bedroom, Donovan describes the delights of masturbation in this speech. He's drinking from a bottle of beer as he speaks and is beginning to get drunk.

DONOVAN. I used to have really clear eyes once. But that's before I started enjoying myself. I was fifteen at the time. (*Long, deep swig.*) My parents spent the night with this black minister. We're Pentecostals, and his son – a right rude bwai, but very good looking – shared my bedroom. Separate beds, of course. The son was twenty-one. In the night he strip back his top sheet and lay in white Y-fronts wanking away right at me. I pretended to sleep but watched it all. He took fifteen minutes to cum. Squirting cream towards me in my bed. Next morning I found him wanking off all over my jeans and he stained the front pure white. He never seem to

16

mind whether I saw him or not, and the room was light enough for me to see him in. He never said a word about it next day at church and I never mentioned it either. But it was very sexy to watch, believe me. (*Swigs.*) About a week later my mate Sticks, who was sixteen, spent the night by me on the put-you-up bed. I thought I'd try the same on him. Just after he said 'good night' I pulled back my quilt and face towards him in his bed. I could see him watching, but he never said a word, breathing heavy, making me think he was asleep. (*In the silence*, DONOVAN *coughs.*)

[KARL. Is that it?]

I know it might sound funny to you, me telling it like this, but it turned me on something rotten that I did it whenever I stayed, or friends stayed, overnight.

[KARL. Same room of course.]

Try it sometime. See what enjoyment you get, or give, to the one who's watching.

———————

Act 3. Two months later.

Donovan has now moved in with Karl as his lodger. He has quit his job and is training to become a garage mechanic. Karl is furious when he realizes that Donovan has been bringing women back to the flat and the two of them have a fight which Karl wins. Karl then gives Donovan notice to quit the flat. Donovan finds out that Susan is pregnant with his child, and goes to visit her in hospital where he discovers that she has AIDS and plans to have an abortion. Donovan is terrified that he too has AIDS and has an AIDS test. When he comes back to Karl's flat he freaks out. Karl takes pity on him and at the same time realizes that he really loves Donovan. The two of them are soon reconciled. In this

17

speech Donovan, who does not usually 'give much of himself away', talks of the ups and downs of his romantic life.

DONOVAN. I'm like that, though, you know. You say it's cos I don't give. I used to give to people, you know. I used to give all the time to people. You ask my mum. But the more I give the more people want to take. Take, take, take, that's all people do. And then I don't wanna give, cos I don't wanna feel, and I don't wanna feel cos I don't wanna get hurt. Candy hurt me. Candy my . . . we were gonna get married, man. It's so stupid. D'you know she slept with my brother. My big ole fat ugly brother. If he was the last man in the world I'd rather shag a sheep. She slept with him to hurt me. I s'pose she'd say she wasn't getting enough. Trevor hurt me. Trevor was the first man I met. Trevor is pathetic! That's one of your words, ennit? Do you know he'll swear to God he screwed me. I overheard him on the phone one night showing off to his friend. I said, 'Trevor, you've never screwed me!' He said, 'Yes, I have!' I said, 'When? Where was I?' D'you know what I mean? He's so stupid! I met Nathan right after Trevor. Nathan was quite nice at first. Then he started to want to treat me like a woman. I wasn't having none a that! I met Susan in Safeways. I thought, I ain't having any luck with men. Susan was really good in bed. 'You don't think I'm a slag, do you, Donovan? I'm not a slag, you know. I'm just really really attracted to you!' Susan didn't hurt me. I hurt Susan. She needs love, you know. I didn't mean to hurt her. I wanned to have a son. That's what it was. It was mainly to have a kid. How could a love Susan when all the time I was attracted to men? That'll only breed anger and suspicion, ennit? And anyway, here I am now with you – another man – and feeling good about it for the first time in my life. I ain't making no promises to you, Karl. But just to be with you, you know. Talking to another black man. Someone who can listen without passing judgement. You make me feel so good.

COMMENTARY: These three speeches show the same character in three different modes. In the first monologue, Donovan is high and full of youthful bravado. In the second, an adolescent secret is revealed. In the third, his confusion over his sexual and racial identity pours forth. He sees everything in black and white terms. He's still young and in the process of having his first genuine life experiences and his first adult crisis. Life was once a rave where all the sexual boundaries were colourfully blurred. But by the end of the play Donovan finds he has to make a hard choice between a man or a woman. Suddenly his identity begins to come together. Notice how physical and edgy his language is. It has a wonderful musical quality and is full of freedom. The actor must note the changes in Donovan's life over a short span of time.

Boys' Life
Howard Korder

Scene 6. A large city. The present. A park. Jack and Phil sitting on a bench. Jack with a child's toy in his hand. Phil looking out front.

Phil (late-20s) works at a 9-to-5 job. He's neurotic and a hypochondriac. He regularly meets up with two of his college friends to drink, smoke joints and generally hang out. The talk more often than not turns to women, and their respective successes and failures in that department. Phil is pretty unsuccessful in his relations with the opposite sex, and his friends are used to hearing his 'sexual sob stories'. At a party he meets Karen with whom he had a brief, two-night fling, and he finds himself attracted to her again. He passionately declares his love, inviting her to go away for the weekend. He becomes increasingly obsessed with her, but she is as screwed up as he is and he ends up not sleeping with her but alone on her couch. Here he describes the intensity of his feelings to his friend Jack.

PHIL. I would have destroyed myself for this woman. Gladly. I would have eaten garbage. I would have sliced my *wrists* open. Under the right circumstances, I mean, if she said, 'Hey, Phil, why don't you just cut your wrists open,' well, come on, but if *seriously* . . . We clicked, we connected on so many things, right off the bat, we talked about God for *three hours* once, I don't know what good it did, but that *intensity* . . . and the first time we went to bed, I didn't even touch her. I didn't *want* to, understand what I'm saying? And you know, I played it very casually, because, all right, I've had some rough experiences, I'm the first to admit, but after a couple of weeks I could feel we were right there, so I laid it down, everything I wanted to tell her, and . . . and she

20

says to me . . . she says . . . 'Nobody should ever need another person that badly.' Do you *believe* that? 'Nobody should ever . . .'! What is that? Is that something you saw on TV? I dump my *heart* on the table, you give me Joyce Dr. Fucking Brothers? 'Need, need,' I'm saying I *love* you, is that wrong? Is that not allowed anymore? (*Pause.* JACK *looks at him.*) And so what if I did need her? Is that so bad? All right, crucify me, I needed her! So *what*! I don't want to be by myself, I'm by myself I feel like I'm going out of my mind, I do. I sit there, I'm thinking forget it, I'm not gonna make it through the next *ten seconds*, I just can't *stand* it. But I do, somehow, I get through the ten seconds, but then I have to do it all over again, cause they just keep coming, all these . . . seconds, floating by, while I'm waiting for something to happen, I don't know what, a car wreck, a nuclear war or something, that sounds awful but at least there'd be this *instant* when I'd know I was alive. Just once. Cause I look in the mirror, and I can't believe I'm really there. I can't believe that's me. It's like my body, right, is the size of, what, the Statue of Liberty, and I'm inside it, I'm down in one of the legs, this gigantic hairy leg, I'm scraping around inside my own foot like some tiny fetus. And I don't know who I am, or where I'm going. And I wish I'd never been born. (*Pause.*) Not only that, my hair is falling out, and that *really sucks*. (*Pause.*)

COMMENTARY: Phil is a nervous self-dramatizer. His demonstration of passion and romantic tragedy gets so cluttered that it quickly turns into comedy. He likes playing the victim and going to extremes ('I'm not going to make it through the next *ten seconds* . . .'). He also likes being on an emotional treadmill. But probably what he likes most is entertaining his friend Jack, whose calm and well-rehearsed reactions to Phil suggest that Phil's tirade is a repeated routine. All of his most powerful words fall at the end of Phil's lines or phrases to give them weight, suggesting that his sentences must build to a punch or what Phil would call *intensity*.

Burn This
Lanford Wilson

Act 1. Anna's huge loft in a converted cast-iron building in lower Manhattan, New York City. The time is the present. Five thirty in the morning, mid-October.

Pale (36) is 'well-built, and can be good-looking, but is certainly sexy. He wears a very good suit'. Despite his appearance and his behaviour, Pale is married with two children. He works as the maître d' *at the Da Signate Ristorante in Montclair, New Jersey. Pale's younger brother, Robbie, a gay dancer, who recently died in a boating accident, had been Anna's roommate. Out of the blue and uninvited, Pale arrives at Anna's loft to get Robbie's things. After pounding on her door Anna lets him in. He has just come to blows with another driver in the street over a 'fucking' parking space. He embarks on a splenetic rant against 'this shit city'. His high voltage personality has been further accelerated by drink and cocaine. His nickname 'Pale' comes from his favourite drink VSOP (Very Special Old Pale). Trying to cool down he has taken off his $250 lizard-skin shoes, his jacket and tie, and pulled his shirt out. Anna is becoming increasingly tired as Pale runs at the mouth and when she momentarily loses her concentration this provokes Pale into the following tirade.*

[ANNA. Oh, God. I'm sorry – What did you say? I'm sorry.]
PALE. Now, see, that I can't take. I can't stand that.
[ANNA. I'm sorry, really, but –]
Well, see, fine, you got these little social phrases and politenesses – all they show me is this – like – giganticness of unconcern with your 'I'm sorrys,' man. The fuckin' world is going down the fuckin' toilet on 'I'm sorrys.' I'm sorry is this roll of toilet paper – they're growing whole forests, for

23

people to wipe their asses on with their 'I'm sorrys.' Be a tree. For one day. And know that that tree over there is gonna be maybe music paper, the Boss is gonna make forty million writin' some poor-slob-can't-get-work song on. This tree is gonna be ten-dollar bills, get passed around, buy things, *mean something*, hear stories; we got sketch pads and fuckin' 'I don't love you anymore' letters pinned to some creep's pillow – something of *import*. Headlines, box scores, some great book or movie script – Jack Nicholson's gonna mark you all up, say whatever he wishes to, anyway, out in some fuckin' desert, you're supposed to be his *text*, he's gonna lay out this line of coke on you – Tree over there is gonna be in some four-star restaurant, they're gonna call him parchment, bake pompano in him. And you're stuck in the ground, you can't go nowhere, all you know is some fuckin' junkie's gonna wipe his ass and flush you down the East River. Go floating out past the Statue of Liberty all limp and covered with shit, get tangled up in some Saudi Arabian oil tanker's fuckin' propellers – you got maybe three hundred years before you drift down to Brazil somewhere and get a chance to be maybe a coffee bush. 'I'm sorrys' are fuck, man. (*Pause.*) How long did he live here?

COMMENTARY: From his first explosive entrance in the play, Pale seems like a wild man. He is emotional, quick and volatile. His words are foul and very fiery. But he is also very protective and attached to the memory of his dead brother. He is as flagrantly heterosexual as his brother was homosexual. Pale speaks in rambling rhythmic riffs and raps behind which he hides his better nature. He has his own streetwise patois which he uses as a shield so as not to let anyone get a word in edgeways. He is sensual and sexual, prowling the room as he speaks. He's a clotheshorse who carries a gun in his jacket like a small time criminal (which is just how he behaves). He censors nothing. He sees artists as frauds. In the action of this scene, Pale is trying to keep Anna awake with his speech. She keeps dropping off. Try to hold her attention with what you say.

Cigarettes and Chocolate
Anthony Minghella

The present. A city restaurant. February, daytime.

Rob (20s–30s) is a young urban professional who has a long-term relationship with Gemma. To the amusement of their friends they do not actually live together but retain their separate flats to avoid symbolic commitment. The two of them have recently been on an Italian holiday with their friends Stephen and Lorna and their two-year-old son Tom. It transpires that Rob and Lorna have been having an affair. On the return from Italy, Gemma completely stops speaking; she will neither speak to people directly nor answer the phone. She just goes silent. This state of affairs has thrown all her friends and family into confusion; each feels in some way guilty and responsible for her ominous silence. Rob is particularly disturbed and the strain begins to take its toll on his behaviour. He worries that Gemma knows about his affair with Lorna and that this is what precipitated her silence. In this scene he is talking with his friend Sample about his domestic 'paranoia'.

ROB. . . . My flat when I got back, outside, – you know the place outside where we leave the rubbish – so you arrive and wade through the armadas of black bags, well there's somebody who lives in the flats who clearly has psychopathic tendencies, really, during the election somebody delivered a Labour Party car sticker and it was in my letter box, you know where the letter rack is, with the dominoes, you know where the dominoes are . . .
[SAMPLE (*he does*). I love that, was that your idea?]
It might have been the psychopath who used the dominoes, must have been when I came to think of it, you have to have a psychopathic turn of mind to use dominoes to number the

letter boxes, so anyway I get home in the evening and the sticker is still there in my letter box, except now it's in a thousand little pieces, literally, thousands of little pieces, which is psychopathic.

[SAMPLE (*agreeing*). God. (*Pause.*) Gemma hates your flat, doesn't she, because of that, because she said the people who live there, the other people, she's always saying that, the Porsches . . .]

(*Irritated.*) There's only one Porsche, the secretary of the Labour Party lives there as well as it happens, she's always doing that . . . there's only one Porsche in the entire building. It's a left-hand drive, it's an old left-hand drive Porsche, it's actually rather beautiful. Of course it's revolting. It's full of revolting people. You know, but it's very beautiful, and it's got the park. When you've been somewhere healthy you really appreciate that, somewhere sane, even fresh air, even that is no longer freely available. Even that's political. My point is, about the flat, my flat, is that with this strike, I'm assuming it is a strike, instead of being careful, the psychopath has lost all self-control and has abandoned the black bag regime . . . you know they won't take the rubbish unless it's in black bags? Well that's all out of the window and there's this kind of deluge of little shopping bags, plastic carrier bags with stuff spilling out, bits of pizza and God knows what, the guy clearly is the Take Away king of North London, when they catch him there will be serious economic problems in the Indian Restaurant trade, and it's all there, the evidence, and each time I get home I want to kill him, I want to wade in to his little plastic bags and discover his name, I know somewhere between the polystyrene and foil containers, between the Chicken Tikka Masala and the, I'm sure there's abandoned pornography as well, stuff which is delivered in plain brown envelopes, there are a lot of bits of plain brown envelopes and stuff from American Express, there will be his name, he will have left his name somewhere on an envelope, and once I've found it I intend to scoop up an armful of this crap which is now blocking the entrance to the flats, you have to climb over it, you have to queue up with the vermin, the cockroaches, the queues of parasites who are racing up the hill to the feast, I am going to scoop up the worst of this crap and ring his bell and dump it over his mentally deranged psychopathic little head.

COMMENTARY: As if to maintain his equilibrium, Rob keeps naming familiar objects in order to guarantee their existence and place in the scheme of things. But these familiar things, 'this crap', also revolt and frighten him. He and his friends inhabit a world where objects and brand names offer vital security. They define who and what you are (a Porsche driver), your affiliations (Labour Party) and your place in the world (an American Express card-carrier). You are the take-away food you eat (Chicken Tikka Masala). All of this identification disgusts Rob. More then once the word 'paranoia' crops up. So the actor instantly knows that Rob's world is one where instability reigns and secrets lie hidden in black plastic rubbish bags. Rob speaks in long sentences stretched out among only momentary pauses, especially at the end of the speech where all of Rob's paranoid fears are infested. He hardly lets Sample say anything except to agree.

Dancing Attendance
Lucy Gannon

Act 1, scene 3. Jack Slaney's living room. Evening.

Reg Dalton (36) is unemployed and down on his luck. He has divorced his wife and let her and their kids stay on in the family home. He now lives in a single room near the train station. 'Been working twenty years and I end up with all my worldly goods in two suitcases and a carrier bag.' He dresses cheaply. He has come to Slaney's house to interview for a job as his companion and assistant. Slaney, formerly the director of his own company, has been forced into early retirement after being partially paralyzed by a series of strokes. During the interview Slaney is difficult and ornery but Reg is not put off by his cantankerous demeanour. Reg is a survivor and in this speech he turns on Slaney as he describes his own chequered past.

REG. I came here, in all honesty – ready to be perfectly nice –
[SLANEY. Mistake number one!]
Your daughter had said on the phone how difficult you could be.
[SLANEY. 'Childish'. I know.]
And I thought, poor old sod. Make allowances.
[SLANEY. I thought you might have thought that.]
I been for some bloody awful jobs. Jobs people like you and her don't ever have to think about. Tanners piling up sheep skins in stinking filthy huts. Incinerator man at the hospital. All sorts. Washing pig gut for traditional sausages. 'Real' sausage, the sort you get in a 'real' shop with dark green paintwork and the name picked out in gold. The butcher wears a striped pinny. I could've done any of them jobs. A

29

trained rottweiler could've done most of 'em. I'd do any ruddy thing, I would. Tell me what to do and I'll do it. Jump through a hoop? Here I go.

[ZITA. I'm sure my father didn't meant to –]

But this has to be the worst sodding job so far. You sitting there like Buddha while she skips around you. Like the ruddy King and I.

[SLANEY. Without the music.]

Ready to do any damn thing you wanted, I was. But just not up to your little games. What did you want me to say?

[SLANEY. I didn't want you to say anything. To be something. A personality, that's what I want.]

An applicant. That's what I am.

[SLANEY. Not what I want!]

I can be anyone. Anything. Workfare. Turn into anything at the click of a finger, or the launch of another scheme. Anything.

[SLANEY (*mimic*). Nobody's perfect! . . . We all have our off days . . .]

Saying what I thought you wanted me to. Say anything me, do anything. One factory closes down and another opens. Tell 'em what they want to hear to get the job, any job. Labourer today, driver tomorrow, security guard next week. Available for any job, anywhere. Maggie's ideal man, me. You have no idea what sort of a nasty sod I am, have you? You have no idea what sort of a bastard I really am.

COMMENTARY: Age and experience are both on display in this speech. Reg seems to be a truth-speaker. He is also very agile when faced with new situations, having held down a number of 'awful jobs' in all sorts of difficult circumstances. But all his jobs have been servile and low-paid, and you can't help but wonder why. Reg is articulate and a master at dealing with difficult people. But what is he trying to hide? How much of what he says is pure bravado and how much is true? Is he a man down on his luck or an opportunist? He is just too available to take on this situation. The actor must explore this character carefully and come to some decisions about his past and present. The speech discloses that there is lots of anger and nastiness in Reg.

Death and the Maiden
Ariel Dorfman

Act 3, scene 1. The time is the present and the place a country that is probably Chile, but could be any country that has given itself a democratic government just after a long period of dictatorship. The terrace of the Escobars' beach house. Just before evening.

Roberto Miranda (50) is a doctor. He gives Gerardo Escobar a lift home after the latter's car breaks down, and Gerardo invites Roberto to stay the night at his house. Gerardo is a lawyer who has just been appointed to head a commission investigating the crimes of the recent dictatorship. His wife, Paulina, was a victim of that regime fifteen years ago. When she encounters Roberto she is convinced that he was her chief torturer, the doctor who raped her and ordered the amount of electric current to be sent through her body. Although she was blindfolded during her repeated ordeals she believes she recognizes him by his voice. Paulina wants vengeance and she takes Roberto hostage, binding and gagging him just as she was. She wants to be his judge and make him stand trial for his crimes. Gerardo, a liberal who is committed to the legal process and democracy, is appalled by his wife's actions and unsuccessfully tries to get her to free Roberto. At first Roberto staunchly denies her allegations, but after much taunting and goading, Roberto finally gives this 'confession'.

ROBERTO'S VOICE. I would put on the music because it helped me in my role, the role of good guy, as they call it, I would put on Schubert because it was a way of gaining the prisoners' trust. But I also knew it was a way of alleviating their suffering. You've got to believe it was a way of alleviating the prisoners' suffering. Not only the music, but everything else I did. That's how they approached me, at first. The prisoners were dying on them, they told me, they needed someone to help care for them, someone they could trust. I've got a brother, who was a member of the secret services. You can pay the communists back for what they did to Dad, he told me one night – my father had a heart attack the day the peasants took over his land at Las Toltecas. The stroke paralysed him – he lost his capacity for speech, would spend hours simply looking at me; his eyes said, 'Do something'. But that's not why I accepted. The real real truth, it was for humanitarian reasons. We're at war, I thought, they want to kill me and my family, they want to install a totalitarian dictatorship, but even so, they still have the right to some form of medical attention. It was slowly, almost without realising how, that I became involved in more delicate operations, they let me sit in on sessions where my role was to determine if the prisoners could take that much torture, that much electric current. At first I told myself that it was a way of saving people's lives, and I did, because many times I told them – without it being true, simply to help the person who was being tortured – I ordered them to stop or the prisoner would die. But afterwards I began to – bit by bit, the virtue I was feeling turned into excitement – the mask of virtue fell off it and it, the excitement, it hid, it hid, it hid from me what I was doing, the swamp of what – . By the time Paulina Salas was brought in it was already too late. Too late. (*The lights go up as if the moon were coming out. It is night-time.* ROBERTO *is in front of the cassette-recorder, confessing.*) . . . too late. A kind of – brutalisation took over my life, I began to really truly like what I was doing. It became a game. My curiosity was partly morbid, partly scientific. How much can this woman take? More than the other one? Does her sex dry up when you put the current through her? Can she have an orgasm under those circumstances? She is entirely in your power, you can carry out all your fantasies, you can do what you want with her. (*The moonlight begins to fade and only*

33

remains on the cassette-recorder, while ROBERTO's *voice speaks on in the darkness*.) Everything they have forbidden you since ever, whatever your mother ever urgently whispered you were never to do. Come on, Doctor, they would say to me, you're not going to refuse free meat, are you, one of them would sort of taunt me. His name was – let's see – they called him Bud, no, it was Stud – a nickname, because I never found out his real name. They like it, Doctor, Stud would say to me – all these bitches like it and if you put on that sweet little music of yours, they'll get even cosier. He would say this in front of the women, in front of Paulina Salas he would say it, and finally I, finally I – but not one ever died on me, not one of the women, not one of the men.

COMMENTARY: This is an openly confessional speech delivered in great detail. Roberto reveals both good and bad motives. He moves from sounding cultivated and benign to sounding barbaric and ruthless. 'The mask of virtue falls off.' He falls in love with his new role. Being a doctor, Roberto is also a scientist. He is fascinated by experiments. But then experimentation drifts into the realm of sexual fantasy and becomes corrupted. The monologue charts this transformation and the actor must go through that process. Throughout the play it is never entirely clear if Roberto is the torturer who Paulina accuses him of being. Is he making up this story to satisfy his accuser or does he mean what he says? The actor must make some crucial decisions about Roberto, otherwise this monologue will sound too general and unspecific. You must ask yourself: am I a genuinely good and innocent man, or a bad man pretending to be a good and sympathetic penitent? This is the dichotomy which lies at the heart of Dorfman's play.

Dog
Steven Berkoff

One act. A street.

Man (30s to 40s) lives between Commercial Road and Whitechapel in the East End of London. He lives with his dog Roy, 'a fuckin' tank wiv teeth!' He has a rather sentimental attachment to this huge and ferocious dog. He is an ardent supporter of Arsenal football club, but he has been banned from the grounds for fifty years because Roy ran onto the pitch and started playing with the ball. He is a heavy drinker, consuming thirty-five pints a night, and spends most of his time hanging out in a pub. He is a loudmouthed racist and bigot.
Roy (8) lives with his master Man.

A man enters stage appearing to be pulling a strong dog on a leash which we are made to imagine, by the stress the actor demonstrates, is huge and ferocious. It's called ROY. *The man is dressed in the mandatory eighties weekend gear: a lurid track suit and what are commonly called 'trainers', a form of jogging shoe. His guts are sagging over his waistband.*

MAN. Nah, e's alright, 'e gets a bit excited, that's all, e's got a bad press, 'snot 'is fault that kid stuck his nut between his jaws. (DOG *pulls on lead.*) Come 'ere, you little bastard . . .

ROY (*growling*). Stop pullin my lead, you cunt, or I'll sink my teeth into your fuckin leg!

MAN. 'Ere, come 'ere you naughty boy. Nah, 'e's lovely 'e is, arncha Roy? You can pat 'im! Go on, PAT 'IM!! 'e won't 'urtcha, don't provoke 'im. Well, that kid 'ad 300 stitches in 'is nut, looked like a patchwork quilt 'e did . . . Well, I was lookin for a tachometer and a second-hand petrol pump for me Ford Transit, so I jumped in the van, bunged Roy in the

35

back and 'eaded down to the Paki who's got a garage off Stratford East, before Romford, just before the A25 turns into the A23 which turns into the A2. E's a good geezer, this Paki, 'We do a very, very good service, costs you half as much anywhere else!' but you don't wanna get downwind if he's eaten a chicken vindaloo the night before! Right, Roy's in the van and I'm chattin' to the Paki about gear boxes, petrol pumps and all that sexy stuff about engine parts when some little kid outside finks, 'Oh ho! The van door's unlocked, maybe that cunt's in there chattin, so let's see what we can 'alf-inch.' Opens the door . . . WALLOP!! Roy's out like a fuckin greyhound, kid's 'ead in a vice, blood spurtin everywhere, claret all over the van. 'ROY, GET THAT JAW OPEN, YOU BASTARD' . . . bless 'im 'e's got a bite like a steel vice. Well, eventually we 'ad to clobber 'im wiv a starting wrench to make 'im let go . . . didn't we, Roy . . . 'e 'ad a sore 'ead for a couple of days, didn't like that, did ya, old son?

ROY. GGGGGGGGGGGGGGGGGGGGGRRRRRRRRRRRR, STOP PULLING MY LEAD OR I'LL BITE YOUR FUCKIN 'EAD OFF!

MAN. GGGGGGGGGGGEDAHDOVIT!! Well, I said sorry to the kid's dad and all that and offered to buy 'is dad a pint and a Mars bar for the kid, but 'e wasn't havin' any of it, 'e was right choked, but I says you don't wanna mess about in the back of a van 'alf-inchin or you may get somethin you weren't expecting, right! I mean, am I right? I mean, 'e can't help 'is nature, 'e sees a brown face peepin in where 'e shouldna done. Right?! . . . well 'is dad saw the truth of that 'e was where 'e shouldna been and so I got the tachometer and the second-'and petrol pump and was a bit upset with all that blood messin up the van. So I thought let's bowl down the pub and sink a few lagers, so off we went and the new pump worked a fuckin treat and Roy's in the back of the van, only I locked it this time . . . right. 'E
36

don't like bein' locked in the back of the van do yer,
Roy? . . .

ROY.   GGGGGRRRRRRRRRRRRRRRRRRR. . .
(*Leaps up and down in agitation.*)

COMMENTARY: This is really a duologue meant to be performed
by one actor. Typically, Berkoff creates characters who are gross,
inflated caricatures of common types. The types here are a racist
yob football supporter and his pet killer Rottweiler. This monologue is a quick-changing double act. A real *tour de force* of acting
skills. Man and dog are attached; one is the extension of another.
But they fight a battle as well. Who gets the upper hand in the
scene is part of the playful tension you must use in performance.
The speech is full of sound cues from that of specific words (like
'petrol pump', 'Paki', 'PAT 'IM') to actual sounds that signal
brutality ('WALLOP', '*GGGGGRRRRR*'). So the actor has to
play both characters plus the soundscape in which the violent
action takes place. If you refer to Berkoff's play you'll see that
these opening moments are the basis of the entire short play.

37

Etta Jenks
Marlane Meyer

Scene 7. A movie viewing room. Los Angeles.

Ben (40s) is a producer of pornographic and snuff movies. 'He looks like a man mutating into a wolf.' He's described as a 'creep' and 'primordial ooze': 'He's like, not a human being exactly.' He is a control freak who hates both alcohol and drugs. In this scene Etta Jenks, a fledgling actress, has come to see if Ben can help further her acting career. She knows his line of business but still hopes that he will help her prepare a legit audition tape. Here Ben puts her straight on a couple of points.

BEN. [I am.] I make movies.
[ETTA. Yeah, but . . . what kind?
BEN. Okay, let's not fool around. You know that.
ETTA. Yeah, I guess I do.]
It's a business Etta. That's all it is. Business. And I want to tell you one more thing here Etta. Maybe you know this maybe you don't, but many of our finest stars made their debut in a skinflick. Okay? That's number one.
[ETTA. Like who?
BEN. I beg your pardon?
ETTA. Like what stars made their debut in a skinflick?]
The world of cinema is like a secret society, Etta. I myself would be happy to tell you the names of the other members, but these stars, these very rich, and influential people consider discretion to be the first responsibility of art. When and if you decide that this business opportunity is one that suits your needs and if we find that you suit ours, within a very short time these names will be as familiar as your own.
38

And believe me Etta, you will be surprised and flattered to be among these elite, now where was I, number two?
[ETTA. Number two.]
Number two, you could make a shitload of dough doin' one film or maybe two films and use that money to start your acting career. Use that to finance your audition tape instead of coming in here and expecting me to bankroll your ass for no reason whatsoever. Did you stop to ask yourself that Etta? Why should I do this tape for you?
[ETTA. I thought maybe as a favor.]
I hate doing favors Etta, and you know why? Because in the long run you will resent me. That's right, you should always pay your way, Etta, and I'm speaking to you as a friend would. Owe nobody!

COMMENTARY: Ben has become so mired in his own slimy business that he no longer sees the grime but just the business angles. But his language is no different from that used by any legitimate producer trying to sell a performer on a role and work out his percentages [See also David Mamet's *Speed-the-Plow*]. Everything in the speech is a means to an end. It's a transaction and not a conversation. The listener either accepts the deal or she doesn't. Take it or leave it, is what Ben is saying. Saying any more on the subject is a waste of breath.

The Fastest Clock in the Universe
Philip Ridley

Act 1. A dilapidated room above an abandoned abattoir in the East
End of London

*Cougar Glass 'is a young-looking thirty-year-old, sun-tanned, well-
built, hair jet-black and roughly styled in a quiff. He is wearing a white
T-shirt, faded denim jeans and dark glasses'. Captain Tock is Cougar's
lover. He 'is forty-two years old, pale, slightly built and balding. He is
wearing a button-up white shirt (without a tie) and a black suit'. Their
relationship is held together by delusion and illusion. Cougar has the
Captain at his beck and call, only allowing the Captain to hug him
while wearing rubber gloves. Cougar dreams of outwitting age and
remaining eternally a teenager. He arranges 'nineteenth birthday'
parties for himself to which he lures young unsuspecting boys. The
Captain helps in all the preparations for the parties but then walks the
streets while Cougar seduces the boys. In the first extract the two of them
are getting ready for the party and the arrival of the only guest, the
sixteen-year-old Foxtrot Darling. Cougar has a cupboard filled with
his collection of pornographic magazines and he searches through them
for one which will appeal to his party guest.*

[CAPTAIN. What does Foxtrot like?]
COUGAR. Women with women.
[CAPTAIN. Lesbians.
COUGAR. The very same.] Find me a good one, Captain.
With lots of pictures. Christ Almighty! Some of these
magazines go back to when I was twelve. That's how old I
was when I got my first magazine. Me and my best friend
stole it. We went to the block of flats where my friend lived
and rushed up to the roof. We sat amongst the television
aerials and looked at the photographs. I had an erection so
40

hard it hurt. I persuaded my friend to get his cock out. I got mine out too. We played with each other. And then . . . then I got this feeling somewhere in my gut. Like a tiny explosion. And I came. It was my first ejaculation. I never dreamed a body could feel something like that. Christ Almighty! I'll never forget it. Sitting up there, amongst all those television aerials. Somehow, I felt as if I was part of an electric current. Every nerve in my body was transmitting particles of sex. My brain sparkled, my hair stood on end, blood simmered. I imagined myself glowing. A halo of lust buzzing round me. The first real moment of my life.

COMMENTARY: Cougar is a narcissist. He constantly uses the words 'I, me, my'. He's so self-obsessed, so cut-off from others that the thrill of masturbating to an assortment of porno magazines is totally in character. He likens the whole experience – here he talks about his first wank at twelve – to an ecstatic religious experience, a mind-out-of-body experience. Also running through the speech is an electric current. Cougar gets wired at the mere thought of his dirty pictures. The language is full of relish and excitement, and the actor must fully succumb to the delights of solo sex. When you read Ridley's play you'll see that this is one of the few revealing moments that Cougar shares with anyone.

Act 2.

In this second extract Foxtrot has arrived with a surprise guest, his pregnant fiancée, Sherbet Gravel. Her presence sends Cougar into a jealous sulk. The Captain delights in seeing Cougar's planned seduction thwarted. Under Sherbet's direction the celebrations continue despite Cougar's withdrawal into petulant catatonia. After the guests blow out the candles on Cougar's birthday cake, Sherbet persuades the Captain to reveal what his one wish would be.

CAPTAIN. Hair. (*Pause.*) I was eighteen when my hair started to fall out . . .
[FOXTROT (*overlapping, laughing*). . . . Eighteen! You're kidding!
SHERBET. Shush, Babe. Go on, Captain.]
At first, I thought it was just a phase. I thought it would grow back. I went to see a doctor. He said nothing could be done. My hair would never grow back. I became suicidal. I was going . . . I couldn't even say the word! I still find it difficult. Once I knew it was happening, I became obsessed with hair. Suddenly, everywhere I went people were talking about hair. How they were going to grow it, cut it, bleach it, perm it, dye it, streak it. When I walked down the street, I didn't look at people's faces or what they were wearing. I just looked at their hair. And when I thought of the future, I didn't think, 'By then I'll be doing this', or, 'By then I'll be doing that'. I just thought, 'By then I'll be . . . bald'. You don't know what it's like the first time someone says, 'You're going bald!'. And it's said like an accusation. As if it's something you've done. Your fault in some way. Something deficient in your diet. And then the accusatory tone goes and it's replaced with something worse. Amusement! And they're laughing. They find it funny. Hysterical. All your suicidal thoughts, your nights of tears, your hours counting dead hairs. It doesn't mean anything to them. All they're thinking is, 'Glad it's not me'. And, 'Doesn't he look ugly'.

COMMENTARY: Unlike Cougar's speech above – a celebration of high pleasure – the Captain's darkly comic monologue captures the anxiety of aging and balding. He practically disintegrates at the

42

thought of going bald. It makes him feel suicidal. The Captain is as buttoned-up as his shirt and severely repressed. The speech is a thicket of entanglements and fears, like a nightmare in which people are transformed into hair. It also touches in the listener a chord of mortality. The actor must capture the notion that time is passing, the body ages and deteriorates, we die. This is a central message of Ridley's play.

Frankie and Johnny in the Clair de Lune
Terrence McNally

Act 1. Frankie's one-room apartment in a walk-up tenement in New York City. The present. Very early Sunday morning.

Johnny (46) is a short-order cook in a luncheonette. 'Johnny's best feature is his personality. He works at it. He is in good physical condition.' He is keen on self-improvement and has a passion for Shakespeare and a relish for language. Frankie works as a waitress in the same restaurant and one evening, after going to a movie together, they come back to her apartment. They make love and spend a considerable time talking and getting to know one another. What starts as a one night stand develops into something more meaningful as the talkative, self-taught Johnny tries to 'connect' with Frankie. She is cautious and tries to resist his heartfelt romantic approach. When she threatens to leave, Johnny phones up a radio station to make a request for a record and sums up their relationship to the DJ. It is his way of making a very public declaration of his feelings for Frankie.

JOHNNY (*into phone*). May I speak to your disc jockey? . . . Well excuse me! (*He covers phone, to Frankie.*) They don't have a disc jockey. They have someone called Midnight With Marlon. (*Into phone.*) Hello, Marlon? My name is Johnny. My friend and I were making love and in the afterglow, which I sometimes think is the most beautiful part of making love, she noticed that you were playing some really beautiful music, piano. She was right. I don't know much about quality music, which I could gather that was, so I would like to know the name of that particular piece and the artist performing it so I can buy the record and present it to my lady love, whose name is Frankie and is that a beautiful coincidence or is it not? (*Short pause.*) Bach.

44

Johann Sebastian, right? I heard of him. The Goldberg Variations. Glenn Gould. Columbia Records. (*To Frankie.*) You gonna remember this? (*Frankie smacks him hard across the cheek. Johnny takes the phone from his ear and holds it against his chest. He just looks at her. She smacks him again. This time he catches her hand while it is still against his cheek, holds it a beat, then brings it to his lips and kisses it. Then, into phone, he continues but what he says is really for Frankie, his eyes never leaving her.*) Do you take requests, Marlon? Then make an exception! There's a man and a woman. Not young, not old. No great beauties, either one. They meet where they work: a restaurant and it's not the Ritz. She's a waitress. He's a cook. They meet but they don't connect. 'I got two medium burgers working' and 'Pick up, side of fries' is pretty much the extent of it. But she's noticed him, he can feel it. And he's noticed her. Right off. They both knew tonight was going to happen. So why did it take him six weeks for him to ask her if she wanted to see a movie that neither one of them could tell you the name of right now? Why did they eat ice-cream sundaes before she asked him if he wanted to come up since they were in the neighborhood? And then they were making love and for maybe an hour they forgot the ten million things that made them think 'I don't love this person. I don't even like them' and instead all they knew was that they were together and it was perfect and they were perfect and that's all there was to know about it and as they lay there, they both began the million reasons not to love one another like a familiar rosary. Only this time he stopped himself. Maybe it was the music you were playing. They both heard it. Only now they're both beginning to forget they did. So would you play something for Frankie and Johnny on the eve of something that ought to last, not self-destruct. I guess I want you to play the most beautiful music ever written and dedicate it to us. (*He hangs up.*) Don't go.

COMMENTARY: Johnny makes sense of his relationship with Frankie by speaking through the medium of a third party on the telephone. Normally you probably want to steer clear of a telephone monologue for use in an audition, but this one is loaded with energy and action. Johnny is constantly trying to fight off Frankie who tries to grab the telephone away from him. The boldness of talking to an anonymous stranger allows Johnny to expand as he speaks and become more passionate with his words. Eventually he is speaking only to Frankie. Johnny is very precise in what he says. He tells a story in the third person which is almost like a parody of romantic fiction. But he means every word he says. He's that sincere.

The Gigli Concert
Tom Murphy

Scene 5. The office-cum-home of JPW King, in Dublin.

Irish Man (51) is a self-made millionaire, an 'operator'. He is proud of his achievements as a builder, having constructed over a thousand houses. He is married with a nine-year-old son. He is in the throes of a mental breakdown; his wife wants him to see a psychologist and his doctor a psychiatrist. Instead in his desperation he seeks out King, a dynamatologist, believing that he alone will be able to help him sing like the great Italian tenor Beniamino Gigli. He is paralyzed by his impossible dream and disturbed by his increasingly irrational and violent actions. When he burns all his son's toys his wife leaves him, taking their son with her. In this scene he is unusually disheveled, 'bewildered, and carrying a hangover'. He has come to King in a state of utter despair and King's reaction is to examine his sexual history. Here, in response to King's probing, the Man recounts the aftermath of his first sexual experience at the age of twenty-two.

IRISH MAN. I was twenty-two.
[JPW. I was twenty-three, clumsy affair – Sorry.]
I got very excited and I almost ran, hurrying home to tell Danny. Danny was next in age to me, I was the youngest and I think he was always a bit embarrassed by my – innocence, I think. He was asleep, but I was proud of myself and I wanted to tell him so that he'd see I wasn't a fool. And I woke him up and told him I'd – had it. And he just rolled over and said, 'how many times' and went back to sleep. . . . You see, Danny (*'There's a story.'*) . . . You see, my eldest brother had singled out Danny as the one to be put through school, educated. But I don't think school suited our

47

Danny. But I don't think my eldest brother wanted to admit that. But my father, sick, and then dying, and my eldest brother had took over, and he became a sort of tyrant.
[JPW. That would be Abramo?]
Mick. Mick frightened us all. Shouting, kicking his bike. Kicking the doors, shouting. My mother thought the world of him. He used to parade his learning too. 'Can anyone tell me what was St Bernadette's second name?' 'Soubrou', or whatever it was. Imagine, he used to give Danny tests. In arithmetic, I suppose. And I'd be sitting quietly, hoping that Danny, locked upstairs in that room, would pass Mick's examination paper . . . And Danny was always trying to teach me – cunning, I think. Street sense. He used to tell me never trust anyone, and that everything is based on hate. He used to tell me that when I got big, if I was ever in a fight with Mick, to watch out, that Mick would use a poker. I suppose he knew he'd never be able for Mick, unless he shot him, or knifed him. But we didn't do things that way . . . I wanted to be a priest. I was crazy, I was thirteen. But some notion in my head about – dedicating? – my life to others. But Mick, in consultation with my mother – and rightly so – said wait a couple of years. And one day – and the couple of years weren't up – and Mick was in a black mood. And he'd beaten Danny that day too for something or other, and I had went outside. Oh, just outside, sitting on the patch of grass. And. There's only two flowers for children from my kind of background. The daisy and the . . . the yellow one.
[JPW. Primrose.]
The primrose too – the buttercup. Oh, just sitting there, picking them off the grass. And Mick come out. What about the priesthood, he said. I'd changed my mind but I didn't tell him. I said – I stood up. The couple of years isn't up I said. But he knew I'd changed my mind and he said, you're stupid, and he flattened me. I knew what he was at, I was learning. That day the priesthood would've gave the family a

bit of status. But, unfortunately for the family, that day I'd changed my mind . . . Oh yes, the flowers. And. I still had this little bunch of flowers. In my hand. I don't think I gave a fuck about the flowers. A few – daisies, and the – yellow ones. But Danny – he was eighteen! – and he was inside, crying. And it was the only thing I could think of. (*He is only just managing to hold back his tears.*) And. And. I took the fuckin' flowers to our Danny . . . wherever he is now . . . and I said, which do you think is nicest? The most beautiful, yeh know? And Danny said 'Nicest?', like a knife. 'Nicest? Are you stupid? What use is nicest?' Of what use is beauty, Mr King?

COMMENTARY: The constraint and arrested development of his life has left this anonymous man – he has no name in the play – in a state of bewilderment. Here he traces his traumas back to a key moment in the past: literally, his deflowerment. Like all such experiences branded into our memories, he can recount his sadness and sense of loss in great detail. Mixed into the monologue is a tale of sibling rivalry, of brothers who share nothing in common. Lack of trust, hate, violence all throw up barriers in the memory scene. The scene begins in excitement and ends in utter disillusionment. What personality the Irish Man once had seems to have been shattered on the fateful afternoon he describes.

Hard Feelings
Doug Lucie

Act 2, scene 3. The living-room of a newly gentrified house in
Brixton, South London, April 1981.

*Baz (24) 'is the national organizer of the UK Frisbee Association. A
Northerner, he is short and easy going though assertive when he wants
to be'. He is one of the lodgers in Viv's house. Baz seems to sail through
the chaotic communal life of the house, steering past all the emotional,
personal and sexual traumas of the other residents. He is well-educated,
successful and genuinely optimistic. He is nearly always plugged into
his Walkman and is a dab hand at rigging up stereos. However, his
romantic life seems to have stalled. In this scene Baz, his tongue
loosened by alcohol, reflects on his life.*

*Eleven-thirty that night. The TV set is flickering silently. BAZ is
seemingly asleep at the table, a half-empty bottle of scotch beside
him. As the lights come up, 'Alison' by Elvis Costello is just
finishing on the record deck. Pause. The door opens and* JANE
comes in. She takes the record off and switches off the TV. BAZ
raises his head.

BAZ. I was watching that. (*Pause.*) Only joking. (*Pause.*) I
must have nodded off. (*He looks at the scotch bottle.*) Or put
meself to sleep. Drink? (*She shakes her head. He takes a
swig.*) I don't think this bodes well for adult life. First sign of
trouble and we all dive head first into a bottle. Still.
Something to do, isn't it? Somewhere to go. (*She goes to the
kitchen and pours coffee from the jug.*) Couldn't do me one of
those, could you? (*She brings her cup and sits down.*) Ah. You
couldn't. I see. (*Pause.*) I was having a dream there. I think.
I mean, unless there was a six-foot naked Amazon in the
50

room I can only assume I was dreaming. (*Pause.*) Spoke to my mum the other day. She wanted to know why I haven't settled down with a nice lass and got meself a proper job. And, indeed, why haven't I? All that fancy education, she said. Maybe education stunted my growth. It's a theory. (*Pause.*) Most of my old friends are married, y'know. They send me pictures. Those little instant polaroids that make people look like inflatable dolls. All my old friends seem to have married inflatable dolls, in fact. If the pictures are anything to go by. Handy for the kids, eh? Last thing at night, you just pull out their little belly buttons and the air comes out. Then fold them up for the night. Very handy. (*Pause. He takes a swig.*) Whoosh. Say g'night, kids. (*Pause.*) Actually, what have I got to complain about? Nothing if you think about it. Good job, nice car. Nice house. (*Beat.*) Nice fucking house. Did you hear that, eh? I sound like me mother. (*Pause.*) Will you shut up and let me get a word in edgeways. (*Pause.*) Most of my old mates think I'm gay, I reckon. When I go home for Christmas, I can hear them thinking: yellow trousers? Only poofs wear yellow trousers. (*Pause.*) I think I'm too nice. I think I'm far too amenable. Whatever that means. Sounds right. Sort of me. Amenable. Sounds like a government minister. We are amenable to talks with the unions, but insist we cannot budge an inch from our original offer. Maybe I should have been a politician. 'S easy enough. (*Pause.*) I'm probably too nice to be a politician. (*Pause.*) Too nice, too nice. Where does it get you? (*Pause.*) *You're* nice. Not too nice. Just nice. Which is nice. (*Pause.*) Let me take you away from all this. I'll let you take me away from all this if you like. Never let it be said I'm not a feminist. (*Pause.*) I think I'm the original little man. How's that for self-awareness? (*He takes a swig.*) Maybe I'm just going through the male menopause thirty years too early. (*Pause.*) I do enjoy these little chats, y'know. A free and frank exchange of views.

COMMENTARY: Baz is drowning in his own middle-class niceness. His life comes across as a blur: nothing achieved, no insights gained. He's a member of a highly educated generation totally lacking in directions and goals. Even friends of his who have married and produced families seem to have progressed no further than Baz. Throughout the monologue he seems to be shrinking until he finally becomes a 'little man'. One imagines him groping for words. Every sentence seems bereft of power, each one fast becoming an aphoristic cliché. He is witty, however, as he tries to bend Jane's sympathetic ear. She ignores him so the actor has to hold her attention.

Imagine Drowning
Terry Johnson

Act 1, scene 2. The front room of a boarding house in Cumbria, North England.

David (early 30s) is a disillusioned radical journalist who works for a popular tabloid newspaper. He is 'a tall attractive man with a dark brooding quality. He takes himself very seriously'. He has come up from London on a mission to investigate a protest at Sellafield nuclear power plant. From a working-class background he began his career as an extremely articulate, committed left-wing journalist but in time 'something died inside him, all his words were rotting'. Now he is motivated more by the lure of a scoop and a banner headline than by the passion of crusading ethics. In this scene he has just returned drunk from the local pub and he reveals to Tom, a local political activist, why he became such a cynical pessimist.

DAVID. When the really bad news began . . . South Africa, 1985, I was there. My first serious foreign assignment. If they'd known how serious it was going to get they'd have sent someone older. Someone like Stephenson. He was there; this Fleet Street legend, pissed old cynic, I hated him. When the worst started there were twelve of us in a hotel television lounge sending out the most fantastic stuff. A dozen of us yelling down the only three phone lines. Runners coming in with eye-witnesses. A fourteen-year-old boy dripping blood on my word-processor, I remember, wouldn't go wash up, wanted to tell us, wanted us to tell. The din, the adrenalin. You've never felt anything like it. Then four days later the lines were down, metaphorically I mean. Everything was D notice. It piled up until we stopped collecting. Material that would have made a dozen colour supplements, let alone the actual news, and no way to pass it out without the actual risk of actual arrest, and – we had the evidence – of actual torture. I was desperate to get this stuff out, but after a couple of days the hotel lounge had come to a full stop. All these so called foreign correspondents sitting around drinking iced coffee. Only topic of conversation seemed to be where to get your laundry done. Stephenson sat there. He could see I was furious.

He put down his glass, and said, 'You hear that noise?'

'What noise?'

It was silent as the grave.

I said, 'What noise?'

He looked at the dead typewriters and the comatose phones and he said, 'The silence. Do you know what that silence is?'

I said no.

He said, 'Genocide. The silence is genocide.'

[TOM. You used that line. I remember reading that.]

It's a very good line. Tight, perceptive, emotive. It had the desired effect on me. I exploded. A torrent of righteous indignation. How dare we all just fucking sit there! We are the voice of these people. It's our job to break the silence! Stephenson smiled, and passed me the phone. We had been forbidden to ask for an outside line. We both knew I might be arrested. Silenced. And I did not have the courage to pick up that phone. And I knew that my life up until that moment had been rhetoric. That whatever I believed or said or said I believed . . . it was just words. I was what mattered. The only really important thing in my life was me:

I once interviewed Enoch Powell. He was defending strong government. He said he believed that man was primarily self-centred, thus incurably greedy and inevitably violent to his fellow man. I said wasn't that a pretty pessimistic view of humanity?

He said, 'Of course. I'm a pessimist. That's why I'm a Tory.' (*A physical display of anger from* DAVID. *Pent up, unexpressable.*)
[TOM. Why does that upset you so much?]
I'm a pessimist too. I find it hard to imagine a world without winners and losers. It's like pissing in the wind, trying to help the blacks, the unemployed, the crippled, sorry, the disenchanted, disenfranchised, the bloody Rainbow Alliance for Christ's sake; the losing side . . . Oh, battles have been won, revolutions have been staged to reorganise the corruption . . . but for 10,000 years the losers have fought and lost and lived and lost and lost and lost again . . . Socialism didn't die last week; it never drew its first breath.

COMMENTARY: It's interesting to see how much David has followed the path of Stephenson the Fleet Street legend: from idealist to pessimist. David's fresh-faced eagerness has given way to cynicism. The speech charts the disintegration of his ideals. But was he a man of ideals to begin with or just an opportunist? When faced with a real challenge of ideals – to tell the world about genocide – he fails the test. Notice that the monologue is full of speed and fury to begin with and then, half-way through comes to a full stop and lapses into uncertainty and silence. The speech encapsulates one man's fall from grace into a kind of living death from which he's never recovered. As the character points out much of what he says is just pure rhetoric. He speaks like a man constantly writing newspaper copy in his head. The challenge for the actor is to turn David's editorializing into convincing personal statements about lost ideals.

La Bête
David Hirson

Act 1. The antechamber of the dining room in the actor's cottage on the Prince Conti's estate in Peznas, South France. 1654.

Valere (20s) is an actor-cum-playwright who has found a new and gullible patron in Prince Conti. The Prince already has a resident theatrical company on his estate and he intends to foist Valere on them. Valere is outrageously self-infatuated and can talk a mile a minute about anything under the sun, especially if it involves him. His vanity is startlingly blatant. He is enthralled by his own cleverness and verbal dexterity. In fact nearly the whole of the first act is a thirty-minute monologue delivered by Valere. In this excerpt he abruptly digresses from a solipsistic rant to thank his host for dinner.

VALERE. That meal! You must have gone to great expense!
How cruel of me to keep you in suspense!
DID I enjoy it? *WAS* the meal a hit?
(*A long pause.*)
He turns them slowly, slowly on the spit. (*Thinking he has tortured them, he expounds jubilantly.*)
Be at your ease, my friends! I thought the meal
Was excellent . . . if not . . . you know . . . 'ideal.'
The vinaigrette: a touch acidic, no?
And I prefer less runny *haricots*;
(*Singing this line.*)
More butter in the velouté next time;
And who, for heaven's sake, told you that lime
Could substitute for lemon in soufflé . . . ?
These tiny points aside, please let me pay
My compliments to all your company,
56

So generous in breaking bread with me
(Albeit bread that was a wee bit stale);
But I don't want to nitpick. Did I fail
To mention what a charming group they *are?*
Marquise–Therese! *She's* going to be a *star!*
No, no . . . I'm *sure* of it! I *know* these things!
So
(*Cupping his hands over imaginary breasts.*)
   'gifted,' and I'm told she even sings!
As for the others, well they tend to be
A little too . . .
(*With a theatrical flourish.*)
           . . . 'theatrical' for me . . .
But, *darling*, otherwise, words can't *describe*
My deep affection for your little tribe
With whom, I do amuse myself to think,
I shall be privileged to eat and drink
(As we have done this evening) every night!
That is, of course, assuming it's all right.
Am I mistaken? Stop me if I am . . .
But it seemed obvious to this old ham
That we had an immediate rapport!
Well-educated people I adore!
It's such a joy to know there's no confusion
When I, whose speech is peppered with allusion,
Refer to facts which few but scholars know:
Arcane, pedantic things like . . .
(*Nervous gulp.*)
           . . . Cicero . . .
And . . . other larnèd oddments of that kind
(*Indicating himself.*)
(Which, to the truly cultivated mind,
Are common knowledge more than erudition . . .)
But I digress!
(*Slapping his own wrist.*)

O, damn me to perdition!

(*To himself.*)

'SHUT UP! SHUT UP! GIVE SOMEONE *ELSE* A
  CHANCE!'

(*He covers his mouth with his hands for a beat; then, unable to
contain himself for more than a second, he plows on.*)

I've had that said to me all over France . . .
All over Europe, if the truth be told:
To babble on completely uncontrolled
Is such a dreadful, *dreadful, DREADFUL* vice!
Me, I keep my sentences concise
And to the point . . . (well, nine times out of ten):
Yes, humanly, I falter now and then
And when I do, naive enthusiasm
Incites a sort of logorrheic spasm:
A flood! I mean I don't come up for air!

COMMENTARY: The entire play is a highly theatrical verse pas-
tiche, full of rhyming couplets, in the style of Molière. Valere's
abundant ego leads one character in the play to say of him: 'He acts
alone, my lord, not in a corps/Of players like our own, where all
take part./His monologue's a selfish pseudo art/Which puts the
man himself above the group.' To play Valere an actor really must
be able to hold centre stage unselfconsciously. There's nothing
modest or subtle about him. He believes in himself absolutely. He
thinks himself to be a wit, a dandy and too clever by half, even
though he's really just a fool, a snob and a critic of all that goes on
around him. Just the sort of man who makes enemies. But he's also
a consummate comic actor who deliriously inhabits a world of his
own making. He speaks at a clip and you really must sound every
iamb and stress every rhyme. This is a role that demands
tremendous stamina and concentration from a performer. See the
play for more outrageous speeches by Valere.

The Last Yankee
Arthur Miller

Act 1, scene 1. The visiting room of a state mental hospital in New England.

Leroy Hamilton (48) is a carpenter. He is 'trim, dressed in subdued Ivy League jacket and slacks and shined brogans'. He has been married for twenty years and has seven children. His great grandfather was one of the prestigious Founding Fathers of the American republic. He is of pure Yankee stock, but has opted out of all the proud Yankee traditions and the conventional rat-race by becoming a carpenter. He favours a simple, austere and Puritan lifestyle in opposition to the rampant materialism he sees around him. He even finds it hard to charge the going rate for his skills. However, the rigid austerity thrust on his family has driven his wife into severe bouts of clinical depression. Poverty is a constant threat in their lives. His wife is once again in the mental hospital where she has been a patient on two previous occasions. The strain of her illness is beginning to take its toll on Leroy. In this scene Leroy is talking to Frick, the husband of another patient. Frick is a very wealthy and successful building supply merchant who recognizes Leroy as one of his customers. He cannot understand how a descendant of one of America's Founding Fathers can end up as a carpenter. The implicitly critical drift of Frick's conversation begins to irritate Leroy who turns on him in this speech.

LEROY. This is the third time in two years for mine, and I don't mean to be argumentative but it's got me right at the end of my rope. For all I know I'm in line for this funny farm myself by now, but I have to tell you that this could be what's driving so many people crazy.
[FRICK. What is!
LEROY. This.

FRICK. This what?]

This whole kind of conversation.

[FRICK. Why? What's wrong with it?

LEROY. Well never mind.

FRICK. I don't know what you're talking about.]

Well what's it going to be, equality or what kind of country? – I mean am I supposed to be ashamed I'm a carpenter?

[FRICK. Who said you . . . ?]

Then why do you talk like this to a man? One minute my altar is terrific and the next minute I'm some kind of shit bucket.

[FRICK. Hey now, wait a minute . . .]

I don't mean anything against you personally, I know you're a successful man and more power to you, but this whole type of conversation about my clothes – should I be ashamed I'm a carpenter? I mean everybody's talking 'labor, labor,' how much labor's getting; well if it's so great to be labor how come nobody wants to be it? I mean you ever hear a parent going around saying (*Mimes thumb pridefully tucked into suspenders.*) 'My son is a carpenter?' Do you? Do you ever hear people brag about a bricklayer? I don't know what you are but I'm only a dumb swamp Yankee, but . . . (*Suddenly breaks off with a shameful laugh.*) Excuse me. I'm really sorry. But you come back here two-three more times and you're liable to start talking the way you were never brought up to. (*Opens magazine.*)

COMMENTARY: A character like Leroy reverses all the strivings towards the American dream. He is simple, direct and plain speaking. He doesn't seek wealth or fame. In fact, he is the complete opposite of Arthur Miller's great tragic hero Willy Loman: a man for whom wealth and success were always elusive. This speech is really a short outburst; a tense response to being rubbed the wrong way. But it quickly lays out for the listener the character's dilemma: he is a man of inner substance and stature who is trying to lead a simple, anonymous life. Only the tensions that have befallen his wife and family make this simplicity impossible.

Laughing Wild
Christopher Durang

Act 2, scene 2. A space in which a talk is about to be given. It could be a lecture hall, a stage, a room, a 'space'.

Man (30s) 'is dressed well, maybe even a little trendy. He is dressed up to give a talk, to share his new thoughts . . . He carries with him a few file cards that he has made notes on.' He 'used to be a very negative person', but he took a personality workshop that totally turned his life around. When something bad happens he now knows to be positive rather than negative and he repeats a little mantra to focus his positive energies – 'this glass is not half empty, it is half full'. His notecards are full of simplistic New Age aphorisms which he uses to cue his affirmative mind-set. Despite his faith in his new optimistic confidence he has to keep battling with his old negative personality. This speech is part of an extended monologue which he addresses directly to the audience.

MAN (*steps closer to the audience*). I was in the supermarket the other day about to buy some tuna fish when I sensed this very disturbed presence right behind me. There was something about her focus that made it very clear to me that she was a disturbed person. So I thought – well, you should never look at a crazy person directly, so I thought, I'll just keep looking at these tuna fish cans, pretending to be engrossed in whether they're in oil or in water, and the person will then go away. But instead *wham!* she brings her fist down on my head and screams 'would you move, asshole'! (*Pause.*) Now why did she do that? She hadn't even said, 'would you please move' at some initial point, so I would've known what her problem was. Admittedly I don't

62

always tell people what I want either – like the people in the movie theatres who keep talking, you know, I just give up and resent them – but on the other hand, I don't take my fist and go wham! on their heads! I mean, analyzing it, looking at it in a positive light, this woman probably had some really horrible life story that, you know, kind of, explained how she got to this point in time, hitting me in the supermarket. And perhaps if her life – *since birth* – had been explained to me, I could probably have made some sense out of her action and how she got there. But even with that knowledge – which I didn't have – it was *my* head she was hitting, and it's just so unfair. It makes me want to never leave my apartment *ever ever again*. (*Suddenly he closes his eyes and moves his arms in a circular motion around himself, round and round, soothingly.*) I am the predominant source of energy in my life. I let go of the pain from the past. I let go of the pain from the present. In the places in my body where pain lived previously, now there is light and love and joy. (*He opens his eyes again and looks at the audience peacefully and happily.*) That was an affirmation.

COMMENTARY: Here's a character whose entire response to life is written on cue cards. His words seem to have quote marks around them. But what happens when he loses the cues and no longer has easy answers? This is precisely what happens to him in this speech and in the supermarket encounter he describes. Suddenly he's confronted by irrational behaviour. First he's startled. Then he tries to analyze it and construct a story, a case history, behind the woman's unprovoked act. Finally he seeks solace by blocking out the world. You can see that everyone and everything irritates him: standing in a line, going to the cinema, shopping for tuna fish. In his world even the smallest encounter becomes a major incident.

Molly Sweeney
Brian Friel

Act 1.

Frank Constantine Sweeney (early 40s) is married to Molly Sweeney who has been blind since she was ten months old. They met at the local health club where Molly works as a masseuse and they married one month after their first meeting. Frank himself is honest about his situation: 'In my heart of hearts I really didn't think she'd say yes. For God's sake why should she? Middle-aged. No skill. No job. No prospect of a job. Two rooms above Kelly's cake-shop. And not exactly what you'd call a Valentino.' He has had a chequered background which Dr Rice describes: 'Yes, an ebullient fellow; full of energy and enquiry and indiscriminate enthusiasms of the self-taught. And convinced, as they are, that his own life story was of compelling interest. He had worked for some charitable organization in Nigeria. Kept goats on an island off the Mayo coast and made cheese. Sold storage batteries for those windmill things that produce electricity. Endured three winters in Norway to ensure the well-being of whales. . . . And he was an agreeable fellow.' His latest project is to help Molly regain her sight and to this end he has enlisted the help of Dr Rice a whiskey-fueled and washed-up opthamologist. In this speech Frank conveys his enthusiastic optimism.

FRANK. Well of course the moment Rice said in that uppity voice of his, 'In theory – in theory – in theory – perhaps in theory – perhaps – perhaps' – the first time Molly met him – after a few general questions, a very quick examination – ten o'clock in the morning in his house – I'll never forget it – the front room in the rented bungalow – no fire – the remains of last night's supper on a tray in the fireplace – teapot, crusts, cracked mug – well of course,

64

goddamit, of course the head exploded! Just ex-ploded!

Molly was going to see! I knew it! For all his perhapses! Absolutely no doubt about it! A new world – a new life! A new life for both of us!

Miracle of Molly Sweeney. Gift of sight restored to middle-aged woman. 'I've been given a new world,' says Mrs Sweeney. Unemployed husband cries openly.

And why not?

Oh my God . . .

Sight . . .

I saw an Austrian psychiatrist on the television one night. Brilliant man. Brilliant lecture. He said that when the mind is confronted by a situation of overwhelming intensity – a moment of terror or ecstasy or tragedy – to protect itself from overload, from overcharge, it switches off and focusses on some trivial detail associated with the experience.

And he was right. I know he was. Because that morning in that front room in the chilly bungalow – immediately after that moment of certainty, that explosion in the head – my mind went numb; fused; and all I could think of was that there was a smell of fresh whiskey off Rice's breath. And at ten o'clock in the morning that seemed the most astonishing thing in the world and I could barely stop myself from saying to Molly, 'Do you not smell the whiskey off his breath? The man's reeking of whiskey!'

Ridiculous . . .

COMMENTARY: Frank is a man of action not theory. He doesn't want to hear 'perhaps' but thinks of things 'without a doubt'. He believes in miracles, has a faith that things can change for the best. He's one of life's optimists. He speaks in concrete details of an intense moment which for him was an epiphany ('the head exploded! Just ex-ploded!'). All his senses are engaged (note his strong sense of smell, for instance). The operation on Molly's eyes

65

is as much for his own salvation as it is Molly's. Making her see again will give him the illusion of solving his own unfulfilled existence. It's important to see that Frank wants to work miracles through Rice.

Moonlight
Harold Pinter

One Act. Andy's bedroom, well furnished.

Andy (50s) is married to Bel and father to Jake, Fred and Bridget. He is lying in bed dying. He is a former civil servant who took great pride in his work. He only swore at home, never in the office. Bel sits beside him and he talks to her about the past. They each remember different pieces of it as though it were separate dreams. Andy waits for his two sons to come and visit him. He seems to refuse to die until he has settled with them. In this scene Bel has just said: 'You're not a bad man. You're just what we used to call a loudmouth. You can't help it. It's your nature. If only you kept your mouth shut more of the time life with you might just be tolerable.' She keeps going on about his viciousness.

ANDY. Allow me to kiss your hand. I owe you everything. (*He watches her embroider.*) Oh, I've been meaning to ask you, what are you making there? A winding sheet? Are you going to wrap me up in it when I conk out? You'd better get a move on. I'm going fast. (*Pause.*) Where are they? (*Pause.*) Two sons. Absent. Indifferent. Their father dying.

[BEL. They were good boys. I've been thinking of how they used to help me with the washing-up. And the drying. The clearing of the table, the washing-up, the drying. Do you remember?

ANDY. You mean in the twilight? The soft light falling through the kitchen window? The bell ringing for Evensong in the pub round the corner?]

(*Pause.*) They were bastards. Both of them. Always. Do you remember that time I asked Jake to clean out the broom cupboard? Well – I *told* him – I admit it – I didn't ask him – I

67

told him that it was bloody filthy and that he hadn't lifted a little finger all week. Nor had the other one. Lazy idle layabouts. Anyway all I did was to ask him – quite politely – to clean out the bloody broom cupboard. His defiance! Do you remember the way he looked at me? His defiance! (*Pause.*) And look at them now! What are they now! A sponging parasitical pair of ponces. Sucking the tit of the state. Sucking the tit of the state! And I bet you feed them a few weekly rupees from your little money-box, don't you? Because they always loved their loving mother. They helped her with the washing-up! (*Pause.*) I've got to stretch my legs. Go over the Common, watch a game of football, rain or shine. What was the name of that old chum of mine? Used to referee amateur games every weekend? On the Common? Charming bloke. They treated him like shit. A subject of scorn. No decision he ever made was adhered to or respected. They shouted at him, they screamed at him, they called him every kind of prick. I used to watch in horror from the touchline. I'll always remember his impotent whistle. It blows down to me through the ages, damp and forlorn. What was his name? And now I'm dying and he's probably dead.

COMMENTARY: Andy is full of comic, macabre sarcasm. He harbours deep wounds about the past. Andy is an authoritarian patriarch who resents the path his two sons have taken. Both are without a profession and direction. He is bitter and morbid. The only thing that keeps him going is a seething anger that searches for targets in the past. Momentarily the speech breaks out of its confines as Andy remembers stretching his legs and walking across the common to watch a football match. But even there he hits an obstacle: a scornful crowd attacking his friend Ralph. We never learn fully the reasons for Andy's hatred and contempt except that it is deep and overflowing. Ironically, it keeps him alive as he splutters towards death.

The Normal Heart
Larry Kramer

Act 1, scene 4. Ned's apartment in New York City. November 1981.

Felix Turner (early 30s) works as a journalist for The New York Times. *He is 'completely masculine, outgoing, energetic' and gay. He writes about 'Lifestyle' and society for the paper. He summarizes his unassuming background: 'I'm from Oklahoma. I left home at eighteen and put myself through college. My folks are dead. My dad worked the refinery in West Tulsa and my mom as a waitress at a luncheonette in Walgreen's.' He has been visited in his office by Ned Weeks, who is trying to raise concern about the 'new disease' (AIDS) and wants him to write an article about it. Felix gives him this excuse: 'I just write about gay designers and gay discos and gay chefs and gay rock stars and gay photographers and gay models and gay celebrities and gay everything. I just don't call them gay. Isn't that enough for doing my bit?' However, just two months later he has phoned Ned for a date. In this scene Felix has come to Ned's apartment. Ned has been wary and caustic towards the genial Felix. After a first cautious kiss, Felix reveals just how he first came to meet Ned.*

FELIX. [You are fucking crazy. Jews, Dachau, Final Solution – what kind of date is this! I don't believe anyone in the whole wide world doesn't want to be loved.] Ned, you don't remember me, do you? We've been in bed together. We made love. We talked. We kissed. We cuddled. We made love again. I keep waiting for you to remember, something, anything. But you don't!
[NED. How could I not remember you?
FELIX. I don't know.
NED. Maybe if I saw you naked.]

It's okay as long as we treat each other like whores. It was at the baths a few years ago. You were busy cruising some blond number and I stood outside your door waiting for you to come back and when you did you gave me such an inspection up and down you would have thought I was applying for the CIA.

[NED. And then what?

FELIX. I just told you.] We made love twice. I thought it was lovely. You told me your name was Ned, that when you were a child you read a Philip Barry play called *Holiday* where there was a Ned, and you immediately switched from . . . Alexander? I teased you for taking such a Wasp, up-in-Connecticut-for-the-weekend name, and I asked what you did, and you answered something like you'd tried a number of things, and I asked you if that had included love, which is when you said you had to get up early in the morning. That's when I left. But I tossed you my favourite go-fuck-yourself when you told me 'I really am not in the market for a lover' – men do not just naturally not love – they learn not to. I am not a whore. I just sometimes make mistakes and look for love in the wrong places. And I think you're a bluffer. Your novel was all about a man desperate for love and a relationship, in a world filled with nothing but casual sex.

COMMENTARY: The fact that these two men have met before in a transient way is finally disclosed. The actor must decide why Felix has taken so long to confront Ned with this information. There's something bitter in Felix's attitude. Like all the other characters in the play he is very confrontational. He provokes Ned with accusations. He's also very blunt about the dark, purely physical side of gay encounters. However, he is at heart a romantic looking for love and hoping he's found it in Ned.

Oleanna
David Mamet

Act 2. John's office at an American college.

John (40s) is a lecturer in English and is up for tenure. He desperately needs this promotion because he is on the verge of buying an expensive new house. One of his students, Carol, has come to see him because she is terrified of failing one of his courses. Her vulnerability and genuine panic elicit an alternately paternalistic and patronizing response from John. During their session John tries to reassure her, mentioning his own youthful uncertainties, cracking off-colour jokes and generally lambasting the whole notion of higher education. Their session ends with John putting a consoling hand on her shoulder. In consultation with her 'group' she decides this is grounds for claiming sexual harassment. John's speech opens this scene as they meet for the first time following her formal complaint to the college tenure committee.

JOHN *and* CAROL *seated across the desk from each other*.
JOHN. You see, (*Pause*.) I love to teach. And flatter myself I am *skilled* at it. And I love the, the aspect of *performance*. I think I must confess that. When I found I loved to teach I swore that I would not become that cold, rigid automaton of an instructor which I had encountered as a child. Now, I was not unconscious that it was given me to err upon the other side. And, so I asked and *ask* myself if I engaged in heterodoxy, I will not say 'gratuitously' for I do not care to posit orthodoxy as a given good – but, 'to the detriment of, of my students.' (*Pause*.) As I said. When the possibility of tenure opened, and, of course, I'd long pursued it, I was, of course *happy*, and *covetous* of it. I asked myself if I was wrong to covet it. And thought about it long, and, I hope,

71

truthfully, and saw in myself several things in, I think, no particular order. (*Pause.*) That I *would* pursue it. That I *desired* it, that I was not pure of longing for security, and that that, perhaps, was not reprehensible in me. That I had duties *beyond* the school, and that my duty to my home, for instance, was, or should be, if it were not, of an equal weight. That tenure, and security, and yes, and *comfort*, were not, of themselves, to be scorned; and were even worthy of honorable pursuit. And that it was given me. Here, in this place, which I enjoy, and in which I find comfort, to assure myself of – as far as it rests in The Material – a continuation of that joy and comfort. In exchange for what? Teaching. Which I love. What was the price of this security? To obtain *tenure*. Which tenure the committee is in the process of granting me. And on the basis of which I contracted to purchase a house. Now, as you don't have your own family, at this point, you may not know what that means. But to me it is important. A home. A Good Home. To raise my family. Now: The Tenure Committee will meet. This is the process, and a *good* process. Under which the school has functioned for quite a long time. They will meet, and hear your complaint – which you have the right to make; and they will dismiss it. They will *dismiss* your complaint; and, in the intervening period, I will lose my house. I will not be able to close on my house. I will lose my *deposit*, and the home I'd picked out for my wife and son will go by the boards. Now: I see I have angered you. I understand your anger at teachers. I was angry with mine. I felt hurt and humiliated by them. Which is one of the reasons that I went into education.

[CAROL. What do you want of me?]

(*Pause.*) I was hurt. When I received the report. Of the tenure committee. I was shocked. And I was hurt. No, I don't mean to subject you to my weak sensibilities. All right. Finally, I didn't understand. Then I thought: is it not always

72

at those points at which we reckon ourselves unassailable that we are most vulnerable and . . . (*Pause.*) Yes. All right. You find me pedantic. Yes. I am. By nature, by *birth*, by profession, I don't know . . . I'm always looking for a *paradigm* for . . .

[CAROL. I don't know what a paradigm is.

JOHN. It's a model.

CAROL. Then why can't you use that word? (*Pause.*)

JOHN. If it is important to you. Yes, all right] I was looking for a model. To continue: I feel that one point . . .

[CAROL. I . . .

JOHN. One second . . .] upon which I am unassailable is my unflinching concern for my students' dignity. I asked you here to . . . in the spirit of *investigation*, to ask you . . . to ask . . . (*Pause.*) What have I done to you? (*Pause.*) And, and, I suppose, how I can make amends. Can we not settle this now? It's pointless, really, and I want to know.

COMMENTARY: John speaks in the style of someone who chooses his words with pompous and painful care. His speech is slow, cluttered and deliberate. Although an English professor, he uses the language as if it were a foreign tongue. Words do not come to him easily. (Throughout the play Carol keeps asking him what he means.) He does not always make complete sense and this was at the root of his problem with Carol: a failure of both characters to be coherent. Perhaps he's trying to keep his anger towards Carol under control. He lays out for her and us the facts of his situation: his tenure process, the purchase of his house, his love of teaching. It feels as if he's on trial and that he is his own best character witness. Digging deeper into what he says, an actor has to decide what it was in John's background that left him with so much 'hurt' and 'humiliation'. He claims there was a teacher at fault. A lot is at stake for John. His career will certainly be ruined if Carol's case of harassment wins.

The Pitchfork Disney
Philip Ridley

One act. A dimly lit room in the East End of London. Night.

Presley Stray (28) lives with his twin sister, Haley. They are both chocaholics; their addiction is so extreme that they survive solely on a diet of chocolate. Presley 'is dressed in dirty pajamas, vest, frayed cardigan and slippers. He is unshaven, hair unevenly hacked very short, teeth discoloured, skin pale, dark rings beneath bloodshot eyes'. Their parents mysteriously 'disappeared' ten years ago. Always in a state of terror and dread, they experience the world as a living nightmare. Macabre and bizarre fantasy defines their existence. Although they are in their late twenties, they regress and behave like children: it is as if the clock stopped for them when they were ten years old. They are like children in a fairy tale: innocents threatened by an evil (in this case nuclear) world. They live hermetically together in a fortified home, shunning all contact with the outside. Presley dominates their relationship, intimidating Haley by rationing medicine and tranquilizers to keep her docile. Presley acts as the historian of their comforting, golden childhood and Haley relies on him to recount key episodes. In this first speech Presley is telling Haley about the one and only time that he was naughty.

PRESLEY. I saved my pocket money for three weeks. I didn't buy anything. No comics, no crisps, no sweets. I went to a pet shop and bought this tiny green snake instead. A grass snake they called it. When I got home I played with the snake. It felt warm and soft. I was scared but I still had to hold it. I liked the way it wrapped itself round my fingers like an electric shoelace. And then . . . then I realised. I could never keep it. Not as a pet. Where would it sleep? What would it eat? Where would it go when I went to

74

school? It was a stupid thing to buy. So I had to get rid of it. But how? All sorts of things occurred to me: flush it down the toilet, bury it, throw it from a tower block. But all the while another thought was taking shape. A thought so wonderful it seemed the only thing to do. So I got a frying pan and put it on the gas stove. I put a bit of butter in the pan and turned the gas up full. The fat started to crackle and smoke. I dropped the snake into the frying pan. It span round and round and its skin burst open like the skin of a sausage. It took ages to die. Its tiny mouth opened and closed and its black eyes exploded. But it was wonderful to watch. All that burning and scalding and peeling. I got a fork and stuck the prongs into its skin. Boiling black blood bubbled out of the holes. When the snake was dead I put it on a plate. I cut the snake into bite size pieces. I tasted it. Like greasy chicken. I ate it all and licked the plate afterwards. When Mummy got home she saw I'd been cooking and hit me. She didn't know anything about the snake. All she was worried about was the scorched patch on the frying pan. She said, 'I'll have to buy a new one now'. But she never did. (*Rushes to the kitchen and returns with the scorched frying pan.*) Look!

COMMENTARY: Presley and his sister live in a world of nasty, childlike fantasy. They replay events from their past as though they had just happened. Presley's tale of the snake is vividly cruel and barbaric but it is also a boy's own story told with innocent glee. Just the kind of yucky tale you like to tell girls. It's almost as if he were describing some tribal rite of passage; eating the thing that you dread in order to consume your fear. In telling this story the actor must experience it as if for the first time. Each stage of the snake's transformation from skinning to cooking to consumption must be sudden, new and relished. The scorched pan is an extraordinary prop to point to at the end: the evidence of Presley's barbarism. All the images are wonderfully illustrated and cinematic.

———————

Cosmo Disney (18) is 'pale with blond hair, and a menacing, angelic beauty'. He is wearing 'black trousers and black patent leather shoes with a bright red, rhinestone and sequin jacket. It is dazzling in the colourless room. He also wears a white shirt and black bow tie'. He works as a nightclub artiste with an eccentric act: 'It scares them (the audience) but they love it. That's why they pay. [Along with cockroaches] I eat other things as well – caterpillars, maggots, worms, beetles, moths, goldfish, slugs, spiders. I suck live snails from shells, bite wriggling eels in two, gnaw heads from live mice. I've even eaten a live canary.' His sole objective in life is to make money. This evening, however, he has been eating razor blades which has caused him intense pain. Driving home from the nightclub he stops his car so that he can be sick in the street. It happens to be outside Presley and Haley's house (see above) and Presley, seeing Cosmo from the window, invites him in. Presley is attracted by Cosmo's confident and cynical manner, while everything about Presley repulses Cosmo. In this scene Cosmo starts challenging Presley about his love life. Once he is convinced that Presley has never had one, he launches into this speech.

COSMO. I hate being touched by men. It happens everywhere these days. In pubs, in trains, on buses, in supermarkets. They come up behind you and rub their hands over your backside. Or they stand next to you, stand so close their knee touches your knee. When you buy something in a shop and the shopkeeper gives you change – if it's a man, he always makes sure he touches your hand. You noticed that? His fingers linger in your palm, feeling you, stroking you almost. Women don't do that. Women don't want to touch. Most women just slam the change down on the counter and leave it there for you to pick up. No finger contact there. But men . . . Oh, men are different. I hate being touched by

76

men. And they all love to do it too. It's because I look younger than I am. They think they can get away with it. They think I'm just a boy. All men like schoolboys. That's why I never use a public toilet. Once, when I was standing at a urinal, this man stood beside me and actually leaned over to look at my cock. Can you believe that? I'd rather piss myself than let a homosexual see my cock. They should be gassed. Homosexuals. All of them. Or herded into one place, like a big stadium, and have a bomb dropped on them. Do everyone a favour. It's not that I'm narrow-minded or anything. We've all got a right to live. But we haven't got a right to stare at each other's private parts.

COMMENTARY: This startling speech is both menacingly defensive and glibly comic. It is full of very carefully observed details. Cosmo is unsettlingly sensuous and sounds like a young hustler of wide experience. Yet at the same time he's repulsed by what he's been exposed to. In the play he's depicted as a ruined angel. He must come across as someone utterly fascinating, even though he describes himself as 'a perfect pretty boy without a filling in his head'. He's also a character whose sexuality is wholly ambiguous and unresolved. Like a lot of Philip Ridley's characters he's completely obsessed with himself [See also Cougar in *The Fastest Clock in the Universe*]. An actor must decide for himself what dark recesses inside Cosmo prompt this discomforting tale of private parts. All the characters in the play hide the injuries of their past. The bits and pieces they reveal to the listener leave us off-balance and queasy.

Playing by the Rules
Rod Dungate

Scene 23. A bedroom in a council flat in Birmingham.

Danny (15) is a rent boy (male prostitute). He is 'small and can look very young'. He has just escaped from a children's home, 'The Conifers', which he hated. 'He has been scrubbed almost bare by care workers, been made to stand under hot and cold showers, been punished in cold baths and hot baths; he has played vicious and wet towel games in communal showers, has rubbed boys down and been rubbed down in numerous changing rooms, he has been hosed down several times in 'The Conifers' garden – playing instead of working; he has even been doused with disinfectant when he had crab lice. In 'The Conifers' they dunked his head down the bog – several times. He has even, on one occasion – two – been roughly strip-searched.' He has only recently started playing the game, but he is a quick learner and his eagerness has brought him easy success: he finds he can earn £70 a night. Danny is naïve but full of confidence and he makes sure that he always looks after number one. He is taken in by a group of slightly older, considerably more experienced boys. Steve, who is 'straight' but works as a rent boy to make his living, takes Danny under his wing and gradually the two of them fall in love. In this scene Steve and Danny are lying together in bed and Danny makes this confession to Steve.

DANNY. In 'The Conifers' there was this boy called Mike. We liked being together. We spent all our free time together and all the nights we could. We liked doing it, don't get me wrong, but we liked just lying together with each other too, and we liked going out together and we liked eating our dinner together. The other boys knew about us, but not a one of them never said nothing. Then there was all the scandals in the other Centres. Everyone nervous. But Mike and me, we couldn't, couldn't stop being with each other. Every day, all day, all night, every night it was all we wanted. He's the only person I've ever loved. Then one of Mike's room-mates grassed us up. They moved him out so fast I didn't know he was going.

[STEVE. Wankers.]

DANNY. Wankers made me stand by the front door and watch him go. Made me open the car door for him to get in. Made me shake his hand. Made me say goodbye. Said it would help me grow into a real man. But I whispered him a private message that nobody knew about. After that, they wouldn't allow me no male friends back to the house. I wasn't allowed to ever be alone with another boy. They said I was at risk. What I whispered to Mike was –

DANNY. } 'I won't ever fall in love with anyone else.'
[STEVE . } 'I love you.']

COMMENTARY: This is a cosy, loving speech delivered in bed. It is very simple in the way it depicts a relationship that is suddenly split in two. No great gestures or movements are called for, just the ability to open up and tell a story. But the story must never become maudlin or melodramatic. It is very factual. Notice how Danny uses strings of repetitions to advance the speech. The effect it creates is of an inseparable couple who do everything together. They are tied. So when the relationship is roughly split, Danny must signal the loss of Mike quite abruptly. Life in 'The Conifers' was a living hell. So this very loving relationship was for Danny and Mike a haven in a heartless world.

———————

Scene 25. A park in Birmingham, England.

Tony (17) is a rent boy of mixed race. His mother committed suicide by jumping in front of a train and he was raised by a foster family. He is

79

not as outgoing as the other boys and there is a 'hidden violence' in him.
Tony dreams 'of owning fast cars when I'm old enough; sexy women;
for little people to say "That's Tony – he's one powerful man"'. 'Mr
King' who pimps for a transnational vice ring has his eye on Tony and
wants him to relocate to Amsterdam. He first tempts him with drugs and
then offers him wads of cash. Tony disappears and his friends and half-
brother, Ape, become increasingly worried about him. After ten days he
resurfaces much the worse for wear and in dire need of a bath, but he
refuses to reveal where he has been, except to say that he has been
'chilling out'. In this scene he is talking to Danny (see monologue
above), who has also been propositioned by 'Mr King', and Tony wants
to set him straight about 'Mr King'.

TONY. You been with King. I'll tell you about King. He's
my punter. He doesn't go with no one else. (DANNY *nearly*
speaks, but thinks better of it.) He wants me to go to
Amsterdam. That night when you and me had the fight . . .
Before that, he took me out and we went to his room.
Nothing wrong, nothing strange, done it hundreds of times.
Quick blow, nothing to it. That night he says to me, 'We're
in for a surprise: a bit of a change. A black man's got style,'
he says. 'He dresses in style,' he says. 'Let's see if he
undresses in style,' he says. He has me take me clothes off –
while I do a dance. 'No hurry' he says, 'I like to watch you
dance.' 'Very nice,' he keeps saying, 'Very nice.' His dick's
up at attention, but I ain't turned on. 'Not interested, you
bad boy,' he says. Kneels down, goes to it. 'Just like the old
days,' he says. On the bed, still at me. Pulls me head round,
down on to him. We stop. He rolls me over. Hands through
my hair, down my back, over my arse. 'What a beauty.'
Finger feeling, pressing, probing. 'What a beauty.' D'you
know what he's going to do now? I know what he's going to
do now. No one has my arse, I'm not a pouffe. Roll off the
bed. Just turn over, can't get at me then. Can't move. Cold
fingers press again. Feel him climb on, weight across my
legs. Kiss the back of my neck. 'Ready now boy?' 'Get off

me! I don't want you inside me.' No voice. Face in the pillow. Feel his hard prick up against me. I won't let it in. Press tight. No good. Greased up. 'Beautiful arse! Built like a cunt!' Backwards, forwards, backwards, forwards. Feel pillow on face. Crying. Why crying? Hand slips beneath my belly, grabs me, rock hard. 'Beautiful arse, beautiful prick. Black man likes being fucked.' No, no, this can't be. Nod my head, yes. Change position then, to get a better stroke. Fast breath on my neck. In he digs his teeth – comes inside me. I came too. (SEAN *comes in. He stops and watches, listens.*) Am I hard now, Danny, telling you this?

COMMENTARY: Tony narrates the sexual act in one long sweeping take as if he were a camera making a porno film. Everything is described as a series of close-up shots. The voyeuristic coupling is full of touches and probes, stops and starts. It's also very dance-like even though it's rape. The actor must get carried away in the momentum of the words which have great forward motion. The staccato rhythm reflects the pain and brutality of the act even though it sounds poetic when spoken aloud. This is one of the contradictory features of the speech. The short and evenly matched sentences have a drill-like cadence. The speaker sounds both involved and distanced so the actor must decide how Tony really feels about this episode.

Progress
Doug Lucie

Act 2, scene 1. Ronee and Will's house in North London. Monday morning, 10 a.m.

Oliver (31) is 'a crafts stallholder. He is small and very talkative particularly when drunk'. He is supposedly having a live-in relationship with the witty and callous Martin. But Martin always seems to be cheating on him. He is a member of Will's men's group where he seeks solace and an outlet for all his anxieties and frustrations: 'A little bit of mental tranquillity is what I'm after'. He has a reputation as a bit of a whinger. In this scene Oliver drops by to see Will. He has been up all night and is in a high state of anxiety.

OLIVER. Jesus, where do I start. (*Beat.*) Basically, I haven't seen him for two days. See, I gave him a sort of ultimatum. Yeah. I know. Pretty naff, right? Standing there in my curlers, with the rolling pin. Not exactly progressive, I know. But. Like. I had to do something. I mean, we're falling apart. Our so-called relationship is just about ready for the knacker's yard.
[WILL. It happens.]
Sure, it happens. Happens all the time. All over the world. (*Pause.*) Will, *why?* (*Long pause.*)
[WILL. Lots of reasons, Ollie. Depends on the people.]
(*Pause.*) When my ex-wife left me, I said, right, that's it. I am never again going to get myself stung like that. Never. I don't care what it takes. I'll never again put myself in a position where one person can single-handedly dismantle my life. Y'know? (*Beat.*) You build it up, slowly . . . (*Beat.*) Like the business . . . I mean, I've put everything into that
82

stall. Even started thinking about getting premises. A shop. Yeah. A shop. Hip capitalism. Well, I haven't made or sold a thing all week. I can't. It's just collapsing. I'm paralysed. (*Pause.*) Martin. I thought, it'll never turn out like it did with Marie, my ex-wife. I won't let it. This is different. Martin's a guy, for chrissakes. He won't do that to me. (*Pause.*) Will. We don't have sex. I know we pretend . . . I mean, it's not that we don't want to, it's just . . . It's another complication. And Martin knew that. The ad I put in Time Out, it said, 'Guy wants guy for friendship.' That's all. All. Christ, isn't it enough? Doesn't anybody want to be friends in this world any more? (*Pause.*)

[WILL. Ollie . . . Maybe Martin didn't like the pretence.] Maybe Martin just wanted to get his rotten little end away. Maybe Martin doesn't give a damn if he fucks our relationship up. (*Pause.*) And maybe Martin didn't like the pretence. Shit. Pretence? Let's not kid ourselves. Lies, Will. What it boils down to. Lies.

COMMENTARY: Oliver is in a state of despair and at a loss where to begin. He's mixed-up about his sexuality and just about every other facet of his identity. His whole world is collapsing, including his business. Each new start is a false start. But he's also the sort of character who is easily deceived. He leaves himself open and vulnerable. Though he talks a lot he actually says very little. Notice that the monologue has a stream-of-consciousness quality as Oliver's thoughts skip from topic to topic. Notice how the whole speech leads to a dead end: lies.

Search and Destroy
Howard Korder

Act 2, scene 1. A booth in a restaurant in New York City.

Ron (30s) is a keyed-up, fast-talking, big-time drug dealer. He spent 'four years sucking bongwater at Hofstra' university. He is married and has a kid who goes to the prestigious private school Dalton. He is astute, cautious and savvy. In this scene he meets up with Kim, an old college friend, and Martin, who desperately wants to break into the drugs business. Here Ron describes how he spent the past evening at a New York Mets baseball game at Shea Stadium.

[KIM. I sometimes go to Miami.]
RON. [You're fucking *crazy*.] *New* York. *New* York. *New* York. Last night?
[KIM. How was it?]
The best, the best. Absofuckingwhatley the best. Last night. Okay. We get there. This is at Shea. We get there. In the limo. I got, I'm with, the, *Carol*, she does the, the, *fuck*, you know, that *ad*, the fitness, amazing bod, amazing bod, fucking amazing bod, and I have, for this occasion, I put aside my very best, lovely lovely product, for Carol, who, no, I care about very deeply. So, okay, get to Shea, it's fucking *bat* night, everybody with the bats, fifty thousand bat-wielding sociopaths, security is very tight. *I* have a private booth. In the circle. This is through GE, my little addictive exec at GE. So we entree, me and Carol, and my client, I see, has fucked me over, cause there's already someone there, you know who, that talk show guy, he's always got like three drag queens and a Satanist, and he's
84

there with a girl can't be more that fourteen. 'Oops.' This fucking guy, my *daughter* watches that show. And between us, heavy substance abuser. I ask him to leave. I mean I come to watch a ball game with my good friend Carol and I'm forced to encounter skeevy baby-fucking cokeheads. One thing leads to the other, politeness out the window he comes at me Mets ashtray in his hand. What do I do.

[KIM. You have a bat.]

I have a bat, I take this bat, I acquaint this individual in the head with this bat. 'Ba-doing.' Right, badoing? He doesn't go down. Stands there, walks out the door, comes back two security guards. 'Is there a problem here, boys?' 'Well sir, this man, bicka bicka bicka,' 'Yes, I completely understand and here's something for your troubles.'

[KIM. How much?]

How much, Kim? How much did I give these good men to resolve our altercation? I gave them one thousand dollars in US currency. And they were very grateful. Mr Microphone sits down, doesn't speak, doesn't move rest of the night. Moody fucking person. Mets take it, great ball, home with Carol where we romp in the flower of our youth. I win. I dominate. I get all the marbles. And that is why I love New York.

COMMENTARY: Ron speaks at such breakneck speed that he skids and slides over the words. His mind is racing so fast that the words are telegraphed in fragments and short phrases rather than in full sentences. His speech captures the high-octane lifestyle of New York at night where personalities meet, merge and break apart. The rhythm of the speech is percussive with words like 'best', 'bod', 'booth', 'bat' and 'badoing' adding stress to the beats. The speech contains a dangerous verbal prop – a bat – wielded dangerously by Ron and, presumably, 'fifty thousand bat-wielding sociopaths' who fill Shea Stadium on this summer night. In Ron's world danger is a daily encounter and winning is everything.

Serious Money
Caryl Churchill

Act 2. The trading floor of the London International Financial Futures Exchange (LIFFE). The late 1980s.

Zac Zackerman (20s–30s) is an American who works for the Klein Merrick Bank. His job is 'to buy up jobbers and brokers./And turn the best of them into new market makers'. He is a wheeler dealer who trades in people. This is the era of the 'Big Bang', megascale greed and the huge profits called 'serious money'. Zac enjoys living in London: 'I go to the theatre, I don't get mugged, I have classy friends,/And I go see them in the country at the weekends.' He is a sanguine observer of all the ruthless shenanigans he sees in the world around him. In this speech he reflects on the play we the audience have just seen in which the murder of Jake the brother of Scilla, another trader, has been the main action.

ZAC. So Scilla never came back.

She sent me a postcard of the Statue of Liberty saying Bye bye Zac.

She never did find out who killed her brother but I'm sure it wasn't Corman or Jacinta or Marylou or any of us.

Who didn't want Jake to talk to the DTI? Who wanted him out of the way?

The British government, because another scandal just before the election would have been too much fuss.

So I reckon it was M15 or the CIA.

(Or he could even have shot himself, the kid wasn't stable.)

There's bound to be endless scandals in the city but really it's incidental.

It can be a nuisance because it gives the wrong impression.

And if people lose confidence in us there could be a big
   recession.
Sure this is a dangerous system and it could crash any
   minute and I sometimes wake up in bed
And think is Armageddon Aids, nuclear war or a crash, and
   how will I end up dead?
   (But that's just before breakfast.)
What really matters is the massive sums of money being
   passed round the world, and trying to appreciate their
   size can drive you mental.
There haven't been a million days since Christ died.
So think a billion, that's a thousand million, and have you
   ever tried
To think a trillion? Think a trillion dollars a day.
That's the gross national product of the USA.
There's people who say the American eagle is more like a
   vulture.
I say don't piss on your own culture.
Naturally there's a whole lot of greed and
That's no problem because money buys freedom.
So the Tories kept the scandal to the minimum. Greville
   Todd was arrested and put in prison to show the
   government was serious about keeping the city clean
   and nobody shed any tears.
And the Conservatives romped home with a landslide
   victory for five more glorious years.
   (Which was handy though not essential because it
   would take far more than Labour to stop us.)
I've been having a great time raising sixteen billion dollars to
   build a satellite,
And I reckon I can wrap it up tonight.

COMMENTARY: Although the speech is written partly in rhyming
couplets (*Serious Money* is a modern parody of eighteenth-century

Restoration comedy), Zac uses contemporary language to savagely describe the gross excess of late twentieth century Capitalism. Here he speaks the curtain speech found in a typical eighteenth-century play: a principal character in the action steps before the audience and rounds out the plot of the play and also provides satiric didactic commentary on what the audience should think. Zac's business involves moving huge amounts of money around the world. In order for transactions to work in his favour nothing can stand in his way. So his frames of reference have a chilling global reach. He's a cynical shark, an icy character whose lines are delivered as cold facts. He'll soon make a marriage of convenience with a female trader and move on to the Far East to continue making serious money.

Six Degrees of Separation
John Guare

One Act. A smart New York apartment on Fifth Avenue.

Paul (early 20s) is African-American, gay and 'very handsome, very preppy'. He arrives unexpectedly at the apartment of two New York art dealers, Louisa and Flanders Kittredge, claiming to be a friend of their daughter's up at Harvard. He contends that he has been mugged in Central Park and that his money and his briefcase containing his thesis have been stolen. He has been badly beaten. Blood seeps through his white Brooks Brothers shirt. Paul is charming, articulate and ingratiating. The Kittredges welcome him into their home, tend to his wounds and give him a clean pink shirt to wear. In the course of conversation Paul lets it drop that his father is in fact Sidney Poitier, 'the greatest black star in movies'. In this speech Paul is asked to describe what his stolen college thesis was about.

PAUL. Well . . . A substitute teacher out on Long Island was dropped from his job for fighting with a student. A few weeks later, the teacher returned to the classroom, shot the student unsuccessfully, held the class hostage and then shot himself. Successfully. This fact caught my eye: last sentence. *Times*. A neighbor described him as a nice boy. Always reading *Catcher in the Rye*. The nitwit – Chapman – who shot John Lennon said he did it because he wanted to draw the attention of the world to *The Catcher in the Rye* and the reading of that book would be his defense. And young Hinckley, the whiz kid who shot Reagan and his press secretary, said if you want any defense all you have to do is read *Catcher in the Rye*. It seemed to be time to read it again. [FLAN. I haven't read it in years. (OUISA *shushes* FLAN.)]

89

I borrowed a copy from a young friend of mine because I wanted to see what she had underlined and I read this book to find out why this touching, beautiful, sensitive story published in July 1951 had turned into this manifesto of hate. I started reading. It's exactly as I remembered. Everybody's a phoney. Page two: 'My brother's in Hollywood being a prostitute.' Page three: 'What a phoney slob his father was.' Page nine: 'People never notice anything.' Then on page twenty-two my hair stood up. Remember Holden Caulfield – the definitive sensitive youth – wearing his red hunter's cap. 'A deer hunter hat? Like hell it is. I sort of closed one eye like I was taking aim at it. This is a people-shooting hat. I shoot people in this hat.' Hmmm, I said. This book is preparing people for bigger moments in their lives than I ever dreamed of. Then on page eighty-nine: 'I'd rather push a guy out the window or chop his head off with an ax than sock him in the jaw. I hate fist fights . . . what scares me most is the other guy's face . . .' I finished the book. It's a touching story, comic because the boy wants to do so much and can't do anything. Hates all phoniness and only lies to others. Wants everyone to like him, is only hateful, and is completely self-involved. In other words, a pretty accurate picture of a male adolescent. And what alarms me about the book – not the book so much as the aura about it – is this: The book is primarily about paralysis. The boy can't function. And at the end, before he can run away and start a new life, it starts to rain and he folds. Now there's nothing wrong in writing about emotional and intellectual paralysis. It may indeed, thanks to Chekhov and Samuel Beckett, be the great modern theme. The extraordinary last lines of *Waiting for Godot* – 'Let's go.' 'Yes, let's go.' Stage directions: They do not move. But the aura around this book of Salinger's – which perhaps should be read by everyone *but* young men – is this: It mirrors like a fun house mirror and amplifies like a distorted speaker one of the great tragedies of our times – the death of the imagination. Because what else is paralysis? The imagination has been so debased that imagination – being imaginative – rather than being the lynchpin of our existence now stands as a synonym for something outside ourselves like science fiction or some new use for tangerine slices on raw pork chops – what an imaginative summer recipe – and *Star Wars!* So imaginative! And *Star Trek* – so imaginative! And *Lord of the Rings* – all those dwarves – so *imaginative* – The imagination has moved out of the realm of being our link, our most personal link, with our inner lives and the world outside that world – this world we share. What is schizophrenia but a horrifying state where what's in here doesn't match up with what's out there? Why has imagination become a synonym for style? I believe that the imagination is the passport we create to take us into the real world. I believe the imagination is another phrase for what is most uniquely *us*. Jung says the greatest sin is to be unconscious. Our boy Holden says 'What scares me most is the other guy's face – it wouldn't be so bad if you could both be blindfolded – most of the time the faces we face are not the other guys' but our own faces. And it's the worst kind of yellowness to be so scared of yourself you put blindfolds on rather than deal with yourself . . .' To face ourselves. That's the hard thing. The imagination. That's God's gift to make the act of self-examination bearable.

COMMENTARY: Paul is a brilliant, articulate and quick-witted fraudster. Interestingly, many of his speeches in the play are about the problem of identity, about phoniness. Later in the play it becomes clear that Paul is a fantasist and a conman. He's also an alienated loner like his hero Holden Caulfield. Paul himself is a creation of his own imagination. None of his tales are true but we never learn any details about his past. He lives in and for the moment. He has played the same confidence trick on many other well-heeled dupes, gaining their sympathy and then conning them out of money. So this is a well-rehearsed speech which, at this point in the play, must be convincing. It sounds like a university lecture. It's an extravagant, imaginative tale full of literary allusions. The actor must entrance and captivate his listeners both onstage and in the audience.

———

Rick (mid-20s) is a 'nice young guy'. He has come from Utah with his girlfriend, Elizabeth, to study acting. They wait tables to support themselves. They are kind, generous and innocent of the ways of the big city. They are also very much in love. They meet Paul (see Introduction *above), who pretends that he is the son of Flanders Kittredge, a wealthy art dealer. Paul tells them that his father refuses to acknowledge him and he has to live on the streets. Rick and Elizabeth take pity on him and invite him to share their apartment. Paul, having apparently reconciled himself with his father, then asks them for a loan of a thousand dollars so that he can get to Maine for a family reunion. Elizabeth refuses, but Rick, out with Paul alone, gets the money for him. In this speech Rick tells the audience what happened next.*

RICK (*to us*). He told me he had some of his own money and he wanted to treat me. We went to a store that rented tuxedos and we dressed to the nines. We went to the Rainbow Room. We danced. High over New York City. I swear. He stood up and held out my chair and we danced and there was a stir. Nothing like this ever happened in Utah. And we danced. And I'll tell you nothing like that must have ever happened at the Rainbow Room because we were asked to leave. I tell you. It was so funny. And we walked out and walked home and I knew Elizabeth was waiting for me and I would have to explain about the money and calm her down because we'll get it back but I forgot because we took a carriage ride in the park and he asked me if he could fuck me and I had never done anything like that
92

and he did and it was fantastic. It was the greatest night I ever had and before we got home he kissed me on the mouth and he vanished. Later I realized he had no money of his own. He had spent my money – our money – on that night at the Rainbow Room. How am I going to face Elizabeth? What have I done? What did I let him do to me? I wanted experience. I came here to have experience. But I didn't come here to do this or lose that or be this or do this to Elizabeth. I didn't come here to be *this*. My father said I was a fool and I can't have him be right. What have I done?

COMMENTARY: Throughout this speech Rick retains all his youthful naiveté. He's also slow to react to the circumstances of what's happened. There isn't a trace of anger over being conned, just simple awe about a romantic encounter with another man. As he says near the end of the speech he came to New York in search of experience and he's certainly had one. And this, of course, is the gullible side of Rick which Paul has exploited. It's important for the actor to read the play and see what eventually happens to Rick as a result of this encounter.

Someone Who'll Watch Over Me
Frank McGuinness

Act I, scene 4. A cell in Lebanon.

Adam (30s) is an African-American doctor who has been held hostage by an Arab terrorist group for nearly four months. As a child he was extremely bright, but his parents, salving their consciences by bringing up foster children, were too busy to praise and encourage their own son. He is confined to a cell with two other hostages, one English the other Irish. He 'is dressed in black T-shirt and grey shorts'. All three men are chained to the walls. 'The chains are of sufficient length to allow freedom of movements for . . . exercise.' Adam is in excellent physical shape, and finds strenuous exercising a way to escape the boredom of imprisonment. He describes their situation: 'We are given a bottle of water each day. They let us use the bathroom, but they go with us. We are never alone. We've managed so far. We are always in these chains, that is so degrading. We are given the Bible and the Koran to read. But the worst of all is that we have no way of knowing what is going on in the outside world.' They are warily confident that they will be freed. 'They won't harm us, we're their most valuable asset.' The three men keep one another sane but the pressure of confinement brings other madnesses. In this scene Adam has been getting increasingly agitated and anxious. When his fellow hostages enquire whether their efforts to cheer him up have worked he responds with this speech.

ADAM. [No,] I hate these shorts.
[MICHAEL. There isn't much we can do about that.]
I want a pair of jockey shorts. I want to wear my country's greatest contribution to mankind. Fresh, white jockey shorts. A man's underwear. That's why Arabs can't wear them. If their shorts don't have a hole in them, they can't find their dicks. I want a pair of jockey shorts. I want to kill

94

an Arab. Just one. Throw his body down before his mother and father, his wife and kids, and say, I did it, me, the American. Now you can blame me. You are justified in what you do to me. You have deserved this. I want to see their faces fill with hate. True hate. I want that within my power. (*Silence.*) Fetch me the Koran that I may read of power. (*He reads from the Koran.*)

In the name of God, the Merciful, the Compassionate.
Behold, we sent it down on the Night of Power:
And what shall teach thee what is the Night of Power?
The Night of Power is better than a thousand months;
In it the angels and the Spirit descend,
By the leave of the Lord, upon every command.
Peace it is, till the rising of dawn.
(*Silence.*)
Peace it is, the Night of Power.
(*Silence.*)
Peace in the house, when the foster kids are sleeping.
Everyone at peace, except Adam in his head. His head is hot. He forgets his manners. He shoots off his mouth. He hurts. Forgive me, my sisters and my brothers, for doubting if you were sisters and brothers. Forgive me, my foes, for calling you my foes. In your good book lies the way to power and to peace.
(*He kisses the Koran.*)
I am come into my garden, oh beloved.
Thou that dwellest in the gardens, the companions
hearken to thy voice: cause me to hear it.
Make haste, my beloved, and be thou like to a roe or
to a young hart upon the mountains of spices . . .
Ah but my beloved, why do you turn aside from me?
I am my beloved's, and my beloved is mine.

COMMENTARY: Adam is a character who keeps himself under strict control even during this eruption of menacing, barbed anger. Notice how measured the words are but how wild the thoughts. His language exhibits a strange mixture of fanatical vengeance and peaceful contemplation. He's clearly been influenced by his reading of the Koran. In playing the character both power and peace must mingle. A series of silences punctuate the speech, adding to its prayer-like quality. The actor must see that Adam is transformed in this speech from an American captive to an Eastern mystic.

Speed-the-Plow
David Mamet

Scene 1. Gould's office in Hollywood

Bobby Gould (40s) has just been made Head of Production at one of the Hollywood studios. He has worked in the 'biz' all his life and his work is everything. He loves the thrill of it all – the danger, the money, the power, 'the ziggin' and zaggin''. He is a survivor in a dog-eat-dog world: 'I'm a whore and I'm proud of it.' Charlie Fox, a colleague for eleven years, comes to see Gould and is trying to get a handle on just how powerful Gould is in his new position and whether he has can get to Ross, one of the studio bigshots. In the first speech Gould assesses his own place in the Hollywood hierarchy for Fox's benefit.

[FOX. You wanna' greenlight a picture? What's your deal, what's your new deal?]
GOULD. What's my new deal, that's all you can talk about?
[FOX. What's your new deal?]
Alright. Over ten mil I need Ross's approval. Under ten mil, I can greenlight it. So what. (*Pause.*)
[FOX. This morning, Bob.]
. . . Yes . . . ?
[FOX. This morning a man came to me.]
. . . a man came to you. Whaddayou, already, you're here to 'Promote' me . . . ?
[FOX. Bob . . .]
You here to promote me? Charl? Because, Charl, one thing I don't need . . .
[FOX. Bob.]
When everybody in this jolly *town* is tryin' to promote me, do you wanna see my messages . . . ?

[FOX. Bob.]

'Get Him While He's Hot' . . .

[FOX. Yes, yes, but . . .]

My good, my 'good' friend, Charles Fox . . .

[FOX. Bob . . .]

That's why we have 'channels'.

[FOX. Uh huh.]

All these 'little' people out there, that we see. Y'unnerstand? Fellow asks 'what are they *there* for?' Well, Charl, We Don't Know. But we *think*, you give the thing to *your* boy, gives it to *my* boy, these people get to *eat*, they don't have to go *beg*, and get in everybody's face the *airport* the whole time. This morning the phone won't stop ringing. Do you know who's calling? Everybody says they met me in *Topeka*, 1962, and do I want to make their movie. Guys want me to do remakes of films haven't been made yet.

[FOX. . . . Huh, huh . . .]

I'm drowning in 'coverage'. (*He picks up a script and reads:*) 'The Story of a Horse and the Horse Who Loved Him.' (*He drops script.*) . . . Give me a breather from all those fine folk suddenly see what a great 'man' I am. N'when I *do* return my calls, Charl, do you know what I'll tell those people?

[FOX. No.]

I'm going to tell them 'Go through Channels'. This protects me from them. And from folk, fine as they are, like you, Charl, when you come to me for favors. Or did you come up here to congratulate me on my new promotion?

COMMENTARY: Gould's slang and shattered syntax throws up an exclusion zone all around himself. It's difficult, as Fox finds, to penetrate the perimeter. The words Gould uses are special producer's argot – 'promote', 'coverage', 'channels' – also designed to keep people and real conversation at a distance. These words give off an aura of power and importance even though they are just meaningless jargon. But the actor must endow them with weight and meaningfulness. Although this is a scene between two characters, it is really a one-way conversation which works best when delivered at speed.

———————————

Gould has a temporary secretary, Karen, working for him. Fox and Gould make a $500 'gentleman's' bet on whether Gould can 'get her on a date, that I can get her to my house, that I can screw her'. In this second speech Gould explains the 'biz' to Karen.

GOULD. [Sudden changes all the time. You want to *know* some of it.] Now, you want to know a secret?
[KAREN. Yes.]
I'll *tell* you one. Siddown. (KAREN *sits*.) Charlie Fox comes in and he's formed a relationship with Doug Brown. Doug will leave his studio and do a film with us. Charlie Fox brought it to us, brought it to *me* really. And in the Highest Traditions of the Motion Picture Industry, we're actually going to make a movie.
[KAREN. Is it a good film?
GOULD. I'm sorry.
KAREN. Is it a good film?]
Well, it's a commodity. And I admire you for not being ashamed to ask the question. Yes, it's a good question, and I don't *know* if it is a good film. 'What about Art?' I'm not an artist. Never said I was, and nobody who sits in this chair can be. I'm a businessman. 'Can't we try to make good films?' Yes. We try. I'm going to try to make a good film of this prison film. The question: Is there such a thing as a good film which loses money? In general, of course. But, really, not. For *me*, 'cause if the films I make lose money, then I'm back on the streets with a sweet and silly smile on my face, they lost money 'cause nobody saw them, it's my fault. A

99

tree fell in the forest, what did I accomplish? Yes. You *see*? There is a way things are. Some people are elected, try to change the world, this job is not that job. Somebody, somebody . . . in this job, in the job I have, somebody is always trying to 'promote' you: to use *something*, some 'hook' to get you to do something in their own best interest. You follow me?

[KAREN. Of course.]

'Cause this *desk* is a position to *advance*, y'understand? It's a *platform* to *aid*, to push someone along. But I Can't *Do* It. Why? That's not my business. My business is to make decisions for the studio. Means I have to be *blunt*, to say 'no', much, most of the time, that's my job. And I think it's a *good* job: 'cause it's a job of *responsibility*. Pressure, many rewards. *One* of them, one time in a billion years, someone was loyal to me, and I'm talking about Charlie Fox, stuck *with* me, comes in here, let's face it, does a favor for me . . . he could of took the script across the street, no, but he came to me, now – I can throw in with him and we rise together. That's what the job is. It's a job, all the bullshit aside, deals with *people*. (*He hunts on his desk, picks up a copy of the book he was reading from earlier.*) Look here. Agent gives his client's book to Ross: 'The Bridge or, Radiation and the Half-Life of Society': Now, *who* is Mister Ross, now . . . ?

[KAREN. He is the Head of the Studio.]

And he has a button on my console. That's right. Author's agent gave this book to Ross. A novel. Written by a Very Famous Eastern Writer. What's this book about? 'The End of the World.' Great. Now: Ross, no dummy, says, of course, he'll read the book. Gives *me* the book to read, so when he tells the author 'how he loved the book but it won't make a movie', he can say something intelligent about it. You get it? This, in the business, is called 'a courtesy read'.

[KAREN. A courtesy read.]

Yes. No one has any intention of making the book, but we

read it, as a courtesy. Does this mean that we're depraved?
No. It's just business . . . how business is done, you see?
[KAREN. I think.]
A business. Start to close.

COMMENTARY: Gould is a character who needs to use a lot of words to say very little. He's in stark contrast to Karen who says only a few direct words. Like a man with a big office and desk, he feels he has to pad-out his thoughts with excess verbiage which Mamet has rhythmically structured in a series of alternating long and short bursts. In saying as much as he does – initially to impress Karen with his importance and power – Gould also discloses that he is a powerless functionary. He has no taste and critical judgment whatsoever. He is really just a money man, a go-between who greenlights and redlights a series of mediocre, imitative projects. By saying as much as he does, the listener has time to assess Gould's weaknesses. So the actor might try portraying Gould as a sincere, courteous people person.

States of Shock
Sam Shepard

One Act. Bare Stage.

The Colonel (50s) is 'dressed in a strange ensemble of military uniforms and paraphernalia that has no apparent rhyme or reason: an air force captain's khaki hat from the Second World War, a marine sergeant's coat with various medals and pins dangling from the chest and shoulders, knickers with leather leggings below the knees, and a Civil War sabre hanging from his waist'. The Colonel arrives at an anonymous Texas diner with Stubbs, a crippled war veteran, to celebrate the anniversary of his son's death. Apparently his son was killed during 'friendly fire' and the bullet which killed the son first passed through Stubbs' body. The Colonel keeps pressing Stubbs to render an accurate account of the incident. It turns out later that Stubbs is really the son whose maimed state the Colonel cannot confront. In this scene the Colonel is fiercely lecturing Glory Bee, the wacky waitress in the diner, who has a bit of a problem with her serving technique.

COLONEL (*to* GLORY BEE). Can't you remember the simplest thing! Don't stare at the glass! You're bound to spill if you stare at the glass. I've told you that a thousand times. Here, let me show you. (COLONEL *tries to take the tray and glass away from* GLORY BEE, *but she won't give it up. Pulling tray.*) Give it to me! Release your hold! (GLORY BEE *releases her grip and* COLONEL *takes it. He begins to move randomly around the stage, balancing the glass on the tray. He spins and turns, leaps in the air, making a ridiculous dance out of his demonstration as* GLORY BEE *watches.* STUBBS *stares straight out, ignoring the* COLONEL. *To* GLORY BEE.) Now watch me. Study it closely. (*He begins to dance.*)

102

You have to pick a point in space. A specific point. Sometimes it's helpful to close one eye until you've found it. One eye may be more dominant than the other, in which case you have to experiment. You have to test them for accuracy and precision, always bearing in mind your ultimate objective. Your specific mission. Always reminding yourself that the human body is little more than a complex machine and, like all machines, can be trained and programmed to fulfill our every need. Through repetition and practice. Repetition and practice. Slowly, a pattern begins to emerge. Slowly, through my own diligence and perseverance, this pattern takes on a beauty and form that would have otherwise been incomprehensible to my random, chaotic laziness. Now I become a master of my own destiny. I can see the writing on the wall. I understand my purpose in the grand scheme of things. There's no longer any doubt. Fear takes a backseat to the certainty and confidence that now consumes my entire being. I am a God among men! I move in a different sphere. I fly on the wings of my own initiative! (COLONEL *spins to a stop and turns toward* GLORY BEE. *To* GLORY BEE.) You see? How simple? How pure? Now, you try it. (COLONEL *moves toward* GLORY BEE, *holding out the tray and glass of water to her. She refuses to take it.*) Here. Give it a whirl. It's your turn now. (GLORY BEE *refuses.*) You don't want a beating, do you?

COMMENTARY: From a very simple beginning – 'Don't stare at the glass' – this sort of speech can take flight. With a tray and a glass of water you are required to perform a ballet and think grand thoughts. Throughout the speech spirited words and movement are integrated. It demands complete focus and you must enter into the mad illusion. First there is the rehearsal ('Through repetition and practice, Repetition and practice. Slowly a pattern begins to emerge.') Then follows the performance ('I am a God among men! I move in a different sphere. I fly on the wings of my own initiative!'). But what brings this graceful monologue to a quick dying fall is the Colonel's flash of anger at the end. He breaks the illusion of the pretence with a violent gesture.

Talking Heads
Alan Bennett

A Chip in the Sugar. Graham's small bedroom. Bradford in Yorkshire.

Graham Whittaker (40s) is single; a shy, retiring man who cares for his domineering and semi-invalid mother, with whom he lives. Looking after his mother gives his life purpose and meaning. His day revolves around her false teeth, her cocoa and her hot water bottle. Their relationship is so close that they could almost be a married couple. They have their little routines and domestic patter which often verges on the romantic: 'I think the world of you . . . You're number One with me . . . I love you.' But like any close-knit couple they also bicker and argue. When his mother proves to be just too much, Graham, despite his meek exterior, can be manipulative and forceful with her. Graham has a collection of magazines in his tiny bedroom which he claims are for chess enthusiasts while his mother claims they are pornographic ones. In this speech taken from a longer monologue Graham describes an encounter in a café between his mother and Mr Turnbull, an old flame of hers.

GRAHAM. Now the café we generally patronise is just that bit different. It's plain but it's classy, no cloths on the tables, the menu comes on a little slate and the waitresses wear their own clothes and look as if they're doing it just for the fun of it. The stuff's all home-made and we're both big fans of the date and walnut bread. I said, 'This is the place.' Mr Turnbull goes straight past. 'No,' he says, 'I know somewhere, just opened. Press on.'

Now, if there's one thing Mother and me are agreed on it's that red is a common colour. And the whole place is done out in red. Lampshades red. Waitresses in red. Plates red, and on the tables those plastic sauce things got up to look like tomatoes. Also red. And when I look there's a chip in the sugar. I thought, 'Mother won't like this.' 'Oh,' she says, 'this looks cheerful, doesn't it, Graham?' I said, 'There's a chip in the sugar.' 'A detail,' he says, 'they're still having their teething troubles. Is it three coffees?' I said, 'We like tea,' only Mother says, 'No. I feel like an adventure. I'll have coffee.' He gets hold of the menu and puts his hand on hers. 'Might I suggest,' he says, 'a cheeseburger?' She said, 'Oh, what's that?' He said, 'It's fresh country beef, mingled with golden-fried onions, topped off with toasted cheese served with french fries and lemon wedge.' 'Oh, lemon wedge,' said Mother. 'That sounds nice.' I thought, 'Well, I hope you can keep it down.' Because it'll be the pizza story all over again. One mouthful and at four o'clock in the morning I was still stuck at her bedside with the bucket. She said, 'I like new experiences in eating. I had a pizza once, didn't I, Graham?' I didn't say anything.

They fetch the food and she's wiring in. He said, 'Are you enjoying your cheeseburger?' She said, 'I am. Would I be mistaken in thinking that's tomato sauce?' He said, 'It is.' She says, 'Give us a squirt.' They both burst out laughing. He said, 'Glass cups, Graham. Be careful or we'll see up your nose.' More laughter. She said, 'Graham's quite refined. He often has a dry sherry.'

'Well, he could do with smartening up a bit,' Mr Turnbull said. 'Plastic mac. He wants one of these quilted jobs, I've shifted a lot of those.' 'I don't like those quilted jobs,' I said. 'He sweats,' Mother said. 'There's no excuse for that in this day and age,' Mr Turnbull said, 'the range of preparations there are on the market. You want to invest in some roll-on deodorant.' Everybody could hear. 'And flares are anathema even in Bradford.'

'Graham doesn't care, do you, Graham?' Mother said. 'He reads a lot.' 'So what?' Mr Turnbull said. 'I know several big readers who still manage to be men about town. Lovat green's a nice shade. I tell you this, Graham,' he said, 'if I were squiring a young lady like this around town I wouldn't do it in grey socks and sandals. These shoes are Italian. Feel.' 'I always think Graham would have made a good parson,' Mother said, feeling his foot, 'only he doesn't believe in God.' 'That's no handicap these days,' Mr Turnbull said. 'What do you do?'

'He's between jobs at present,' Mother said. 'He used to do soft toys for handicapped children. Then he was making paper flowers at one stage.' I went to the toilet.

COMMENTARY: The speech is full of local colour and very specific details down to 'the chip in the sugar'. The situation described is that of two suitors out on a date with the same woman. The mother and Mr Turnbull are critical of Graham and talk about him as if he were not there. Graham himself wishes he weren't. Gradually it emerges that Mr Turnbull is leading the mother on and is not the man he pretends to be. Graham is both her confidant and also a son caught in the middle of a messy relationship. You can hear in the speech that he is reticent, shy and silent. He doesn't fight back but he is sly and vengeful in the way he remembers and portrays emotion-laden events. He's also a terrible snob. Everything about Mr Turnbull irritates and appalls him.

Three Hotels
Jon Robin Baitz

Part One: The Halt & the Lame. A hotel suite in Tangier, Morocco.

Kenneth Hoyle (40s–50s) is a rising vice-president with an American multinational corporation which sells baby formula to the Third World. His company particularly values him because he is 'good at firing people' and they have sent him to Tangier to sack the local staff. Hoyle has on 'a rather exquisite summer suit' and he is drinking martinis. Although he has lived and breathed the corporate way all his life, he is beginning to have doubts about the ethics of his job as he discloses in this speech.

HOYLE. My first year of this particular assignment consisted almost exclusively of getting off of prop planes and doing 'that sort of work'. Because by the time Mulcahey and Kroener finally decided to let me have a shot at it, the orange bits on the lucite map had pretty much occluded our blue. And I was a sort of last-ditch-try-*anything*-what-about-*Hoyle* sort of a thing.

The result has been a bit of a bloodbath. People who used to want to have a drink . . . they shy away a bit now. Do I blame them? You can't. Even though I don't make a game of it or take the slightest bit of pleasure out of the task. What sort of person would? But the thing to do is do it quickly. Because when you linger it's sheer hell.

In less than an hour the next batch starts trudging in. Less than an hour, next batch. (*Another martini is mixed.*) This is how it's done. 'Varney. It's no accident that I'm stopping off here in Tangier.' And he looks at me. At first there is this
108

moment of denial. The raw animal response – the instinct – 'Do I run, do I hide?' (HOYLE *is quiet for a moment.*) And I'll just sit very quietly. Because I want him to understand the thing that is happening and to create *an atmosphere of dignity.* Which is up to them. Before I have to utter the unfortunate words, 'I'm here because we have to make a change.' It's so much better when the words are not actually spoken.

But Varney, he gets it, he's an old hand. You know when it's over. So we sit here quietly. And then he asks me, 'Doesn't it feel odd, Ken?'

'What?' I say.

And he says, 'Your rise to power, Ken.' And then he goes. Quietly goes. They go quietly when I do it.

And afterwards, when one is sitting by oneself here in one's room, it is not hard to think of the railroad tracks to the ovens.

You do not want to talk about the ovens at World Headquarters. One time in the War Room, I made one of my little asides. I said I hoped that our baby-formula marketing policy in the Third World would not be looked upon as some sort of horrifying mercantile . . . Final Solution in twenty years. And Kroener looked at me over this huge table we have and said in his Havanaesque accent, 'Well I hardly see the comparison between baby formula and Zyclon B gas, do you?' Barks out a laugh. Which shuts *me* up. Quickly. Let me tell you.

COMMENTARY: Hoyle is a master of corporate language and clichés. He's also mastered the clear-headed probity of a corporate strategist. Communication is by means of telegraphed messages. His language is rigidly controlled and you have to look for points where Hoyle shows stress ('Because when you linger it's sheer hell.') A side of him sounds like a hired assassin confessing his crimes. His job is to come in, reduce employees and then leave. But Hoyle's conscience is beginning to bother him. Corporate affairs are becoming mixed up with the holocaust. The citadel of power – World Headquarters – is no longer a safe haven. People are beginning to ask questions about motives. Hoyle himself is one of the probers. There is also a tough, mean side to Hoyle which he is proud to reveal.

To
Jim Cartwright

One Act. A pub in the North of England.

Landlord (40s) runs the pub with his wife. He is a genial and solicitous host with an easy line in chatter. He is always very concerned about money and the bottom line in his bustling pub. He and his wife have a bitter and taunting relationship. In this speech he gives the audience a taste of the life of a landlord.

LANDLORD (*turns to audience*). First night in here? Well, you'll get used to us. We're a lively pub. It's calmed down a bit now, but it comes in waves. Not going to ask you what you're doing here, never do, that's one of our few rules. We get a lot of rendezvousers here you see, but we're also strong on couples, don't get me wrong. They either come in pairs or end up that way. That woman over there is my wife, bitch. I run this place virtually on my own. We've been here bloody years. In fact we met outside this pub when we were kids, me and cow. Too young to get in, snotty conked, on tip-toes peeking through the frosted windows. We had our first drink in here, we courted in here, we had our twenty first's in here, we had our wedding reception here, and now we own the bloody place. I only did it for her, it's what she'd always wanted. Done some knocking through recently, got the walls down, made it all into one. You can get around better, and more eyes can meet across a crowded room. Better that, better for business and pleasure and for keeping an eye on that roving tart. Where is she with them glasses? Wouldn't mind a bloody drink meself, I'll have one later.

It's a constant battle keeping your throat away from the stock. It really is the landlord's last temptation. Because this is it for us proprietors. This is our life, these bar sides, to them wall sides and that's it. People and pints and measures and rolling out the bloody barrel. Working and social life all mixtured, a cocktail you can't get away from. Until night when we fall knackered to bed. But I'm not complaining, no, no. As long as many mouths are clacking at many glasses and the tills keep on a singing. What more could a publican want?

COMMENTARY: This is a two-character play in which the two performers play a variety of roles. The Landlord has to establish the convention that the audience is in a busy pub full of noise and comings and goings. As he tells us his story he keeps his eyes on all the activity around him. What he tells us is probably a well-rehearsed script he has told in confidence to dozens of customers before. All the phrases are just too well-honed. He also manages to encapsulate a relationship with his wife which will become one of the central motifs of the play. The speech is full of physical gestures and interaction. The actor has to create a world and then inhabit it with this monologue.

Moth (40) comes to the pub before his girlfriend Maudie arrives. He is a compulsive flirt and drives Maudie to distraction, 'Look at your eyes, they're everywhere, up every skirt, along every leg, round every bra rim. Why oh why do you keep chasing women?' However, with all this chasing he never actually gets off with any of the girls. Despite his brash confidence, he knows all too well that he is a loser and confides to Maudie: 'I'm losing everything, my flair, my waistline, what's next to go – you?' In this speech he is taking the opportunity to chat up a girl at the bar.

Lights pick up MOTH *chatting a young woman up. Imaginary or real from the audience.*

MOTH. You're beautiful you. You're absolutely beautiful you. Look at you. You're fantastic you. I love you. I love the bones of you. I do. You think it's too quick don't you. But you can't see yourself. You're just . . . I'm in love with you, I'm not joking. I've seen some women, but you. Let's get back to what you are, beautiful. Did you just smile then or did someone turn the lights on? You are beautiful you. You stand for beauty. You sit for it too. Look how you sit you, like a glamour model that's how. You . . . You're quiet though, but I love that in a girl, love that, don't get me wrong. You're beauty you. Beauty itself. Beauty is you. You're marvellous as well as being beautiful too, you. Yes, too good for this place I'll tell you that. What's a beautiful girl like you doing in a place like this, or whatever they say, is that what they say, who cares, who cares now, eh? You are a star, and you don't even know it. A star before you start. Everything about you's, just . . . You are it. The beauty of all times. You're just beautiful and that's it! Done, finished, it. Because you are the most beautiful thing ever brought to this earth. And you're for me you. You are for me. There's no bones about it, none! Here's the back of my hand, here, here. And here's the pen, number, number please, number, before I stop breathing.

COMMENTARY: Moth is a down-market Don Juan. He flutters around women who attract him like a flame. But he's got a very good line of romantic banter though what he says sounds like the lyrics from dozens of torch songs. Every line is carefully targeted and released for maximum effect. He tells a woman exactly what he thinks she wants to hear. The speech works by exaggerated expansion: each line is topped by the next. Notice that the rhyming focus is always on 'you, you, you'. The actor must never let the listener get a word in edgeways otherwise it may be a rejection. Moth also moves with his words, it is as if his body and tongue are never still.

Two Shakespearean Actors
Richard Nelson

Act 1, scene 7. A private drawing room in a New York hotel. One a.m. May 1849.

William Charles Macready (50s) is the great English actor who is on tour through America with his theatre company. He is vain, arrogant and quite evidently not in his prime. He is performing his version of Macbeth at the Astor Place Theatre at the same time as the premier American actor Edwin Forrest is presenting his version of the Scottish Play at the Broadway Theatre. There is an intense rivalry between the two actors and a radical difference in their approaches to the actor's craft and technique. Macredy gives primacy to the voice and text, while Forrest favours emotion and character. Macready is also twenty years older than Forrest. At a party given by the playwright Dion Boucicault, Macready and Forrest are holding forth on their respective approaches to acting. Macready, who has been drinking heavily, launches forth with this speech when prompted by Forrest's direct question of 'Why do you act?'.

MACREADY. It's hard to explain really. Where shall I begin? (*Beat.*) You see – as Descartes has said – inside us all are these – . He called them animal spirits. (*Beat.*) Which are really, what other people call – passions. (*Short pause. FORREST nods.*) And they're all – these spirits – they're bordered, they're all sort of fenced in. (*Suddenly remembering.*) You could also call them *emotions*. (*Beat.*) Anyway, they're fenced in. But when one of them escapes from the others – . And is not quickly caught by – . I don't know, spirits who do the catching, like sheep-dogs catch – . (*Beat.*) [FORREST. Sheep.]

115

That's right. Like sheep-dogs catch sheep. Anyway, when one escapes and is not caught, then it becomes a very deep, a very – . A very passionate – . (*Beat.*) What?! (*Beat. Remembers.*) Feeling! Feeling. (*Short pause.*) So what an actor does – I believe – is this: philosophically speaking – . I haven't studied enough philosophy – . I'd like to study much much more, but – . Well – . People like us who are busy *doing* – ! But, as I was saying, the art of the actor – . (*Beat.*) What was I going to say? I was about to say something that was very clear. I remember. The art of the actor is like ripping down the fences. (*Beat.*) And tying up the sheep-dogs. (*Beat.*) And letting the spirits loose. A few at a time. Or more! Depending on the part. Letting them roam for a while. (*Short pause.*) So, that's what I love about acting. (*Pause*).) I don't know how clear I've been.

COMMENTARY: Perhaps the question of why he acts has never been asked of Macready. He certainly doesn't have a series of pat answers. Talking about passions, emotions and feelings does not come easily to him. He's all penned in. He sounds as if he's wandered into alien territory. Every phrase is an avoidance. He's an actor without a script. Onstage he is normally eloquent and fluid. Here he is halting and searches for the right words which never come. Though drunk he desperately tries to sound sober.

A Wholly Healthy Glasgow
Iain Heggie

Act 1. The massage chambers of the Spartan Health Club, Glasgow.

Charley Hood (30s) is the senior gym instructor at the Spartan Health Club owned by Bobby Bybugger. The club has the following sales arrangements: 'A new enrollment *is a new club member who has* enrolled for one year. An early cheap rate renewal *is a special offer. Existing members are offered a second year's membership at a reduced rate by taking it out well in advance of expiration. Sales staff are paid a commission by the company for new enrollments and early renewals. They are therefore tempted to try to renew members as soon as possible after enrollment.' Charley hard sells subscriptions to the punters and passes them on to Donald Dick who offers 'après massage nooky' to their clients. They have worked together as a team for several years, and their rather dubious technique has been well-hidden from their boss who is based in Pontefract. Alana, the receptionist and Charley's sometime girlfriend, also uses the club to pick up clients. Charley and his colleagues all use the club for their own dubious ends. Charley works to get his 'renewals' as he says 'I discover this talent I've got for enrolling, renewing in practically the same bastarding breath. So OK I admit it: I totally ignore the six-visits rule.' In this scene Donald has just revealed that he has lined up his own punter. This throws Charley into a rage because it goes against their professional 'agreement'. In this speech Charley sets Donald straight about the way they do business.*

CHARLEY. Well ra ha ha. Aye ra ha ha and don't *come* it. *Have you fuck* lined yourself up a line up. Because that's not the arrangement. And. You *couldn't line yourself up a line up. Because let's face it about you Donny, you are nothing but a / lined your own* line up? Because for *fuck's* sake . . .

(CHARLEY *takes a puff*.) And. Now. But. Donny my boy, son. See fucking here. Time to acquaint ourselves the *bastarding business* aspect, eh? So last day the month's the day. And. Club's £100 short the break even. And. Meaning. I'm £100 short my bonus. And. So my bonus is not shiting much. (I can forego that bastard, no bother.) And. But we get by the break even we keep jobbying Bobby quiet. (A fact or a falsehood?) And. Meaning: We catch this certain to renew his membership beauty of a bastarding renewal punter due in any minute. And. Because he's *the only* certain-to-renew-his-membership beauty of a bastarding renewal punter's going to barge in with a cheque book all night. And. We get by the break even if it stops Bobby coming from Pontefract. And. Because Bobby coming from Pontefract puts the boot *right up* all that you, me have built up together over the years. (Am I right, am I wrong?) And. So howsabout just holding on to my giant jobby of a certain to renew his membership beauty of a bastarding renewal punter ten minutes at reception for us, uh? Alana, me'll be trying on a couple of patched up badgers. So I'll see she doesn't exceed a swagger round the bar, the Empire Hotel in them. And. So ra ha ha and nip back in here, so I will, pin down the renewal boy and knock the cash up by the break even. (Brilliant arrangement, uh?) And. Who's Bobby think he's kidding? Because I says to Bobby. I says: 'No chance breaking even in August, Bobby. Glasgow's evacuated to the Costa Brava. Glasgow's eyeing up suntanned talent out a hotel balcony telescope at Corfu. Glasgow's chucking up Paella down on a Majorcan stank.' (*Pause*.) And he listen? He fuck. And. So take over reception from my Alana, uh?

COMMENTARY: Charley uses his own special argot. It's full of the convoluted transactions that make the world of the Spartan Health

118

Club seem so outrageous. It's never actually clear whether or not he ever steps in the gym because he sounds as if he's only on the lookout for new punters. Charley's words capture the smarmy, unhealthy life in this underworld. He obviously understands everything he's saying which is the source of the comedy. Because to the listener what he says sounds like complete nonsense and double-talk. The Scottish accent and local phrases add dash and colour to the monologue. The actor must understand every twist and turn of Charley's bizarre reasoning because Charley is actually trying to be very clear and specific. It's a speech of explanation, of 'meaning'. Charley is always selling. His whole livelihood is threatened should the owner of the club get wind of what's going on.

———————

Donald Dick (40s) is a gay masseur at the Spartan Health Club. Every punter that Charley lines up is a new source of 'après-massage nooky' for Donald: as he says '. . . not only am I bent . . . I'm bent on the premises . . . see me . . . I am one the lowest quality cunts the world. Because there is not one guy going I haven't had my hand well down his trousers. (On the premises.)' His massage technique he describes as follows: 'It is fuck therapy. It's a pornophallic half-baked grope the dark, you don't know what hot wet object you'll put your hand on next.' His promiscuity is rampant and he seeks 'nooky' wherever he goes. In this speech from Act Two Donald describes an encounter with the porter at the nearby Empire hotel.

DONALD. Reception.
[CHARLEY. Eh? Can a guy get to know what gives?]
Reception, the Empire Hotel.
[CHARLEY. Reception, the Empire Hotel?
DONALD. Yes. (*Pause.*)
CHARLEY. What for? You looked up, you looked down the signing in sheet reception, the Empire Hotel *what for?*]
I've to avoid the porter.

[CHARLEY. The porter? Oh for fuck's sake, Donny. *What's going on?*]

Because it's more than my life's worth to *not* avoid the porter, the Empire Hotel. Did I not tell you about this, Charley? I could've *sworn* I told you about this. I meant to. (Sorry.) Well. Several weeks ago, right? I'm standing the bar, the Empire Hotel. This guy comes up to me. He comes up to me, he goes, 'Follow me, uh?' So I follow him out the lobby. I'm out the lobby, he's standing the lift, the back, the lift, coming across the flagrant come on. I thought. 'Fuck'. (You know.) I goes in the lift, he shuts the door, we go up, he stops it. He stops it? He *jams* it between floors. He goes, 'Take your dick out.' I goes, 'Pardon?' He goes, 'Take your dick out and *come on.*' I goes, 'What?' He goes, 'You head.' I goes, 'OK.' So after the wee episode we come out the lift *past half the bastarding staff* the Empire Hotel waiting to *get in* the lift. And. Some wise cunt goes, 'Could you credit the depths this porter guy will stoop to? Because imagine going with *that.*' So 'that' Charley is *me*. I mean: *me*? I've had *coachloads* of porters after *me* in *my* time. (Fuck.) And you want to see the uncouth the youth to me *ever since*. So see this porter, the Empire Hotel, right? I'm avoiding him . . . Sorry but that's it.

COMMENTARY: This sexual encounter is described like a French farce. It is full of comings and goings and fumblings. It's a real quickie, over before it's barely begun. Donald Dick's life is full of dicks. Like a stand-up comic, he's a master of the briefly told tale. All the action is encapsulated in short, sharp sentences. His accent adds a dash of colour and spice to what he says.

The Woman Who Cooked her Husband
Debbie Isitt

Scene 4. Suspicion. Somewhere near Liverpool, England.

Kenneth (40s) is married to Hilary. He is an aging Teddy boy with a passion for Elvis Presley. 'His costume is a green taffeta drape coat with black drainpipe trousers.' After nineteen years of marriage, Kenneth has started having a clandestine affair with Laura. He is afraid of approaching middle age and this affair makes him feel that 'I can put it off for a good few years, I'm starting again and I feel just like a teenager.' In this scene Kenneth has been lying about why he has to go out that evening and he is convinced that Hilary must know about the affair. The excuse he gives for going out is to meet a mate and work on his car's suspension.

KENNETH. You've got a screw loose, you have – you're losing your mind!! Just leave me alone – get off my back – go and get some professional help and don't talk to me until you're well! It's like living with a lunatic – you want to be careful. I'll have you certified!! (*Spotlight on* KENNETH.) She knows!!! I know she knows – I answered too quickly – 'the suspension', I said straight off – I should have hesitated – maybe if I said something more convincing – like the fan belt – I don't know – how could she – we've been so discreet – my life's over – that's it – I'm finished! How could I have been so stupid? I should have told her straight – if you're implying something Hilary – just come out and say it – I assure you I've got nothing to hide – I should have laughed it off – said she has a warped sense of humour – but how could I – she never actually accused me of anything – it was indirect – cunning, but that's not like her – maybe she doesn't know – maybe I'm getting paranoid – course she doesn't – how could she? Oh, relief! It was just my conscience making me think – ha ha ha ha – but what if she does? We'll just have to be more careful – just in case – take extra precautions – I've had a bad scare, but there's nothing she can prove – so relax – calm down, in the future be more reassuring – be nicer to her, buy some flowers – women and flowers, the answer to all their fears – that's the sort of stuff she needs – pay her more compliments – not from the heart, Laura, just from the brain – it's best all round if I tell her in my own time – not let her find out – I can't stand the thought all the screaming hysterics – all that weeping and throwing plates, all the accusing looks and hard done by speeches – we need to be very, very secretive – what she don't know, won't hurt her. Good, good, I feel better now. The things I go through for you, I hope you appreciate it.

COMMENTARY: Kenneth explains his total motivation to the audience. He confides in us. All his fears and anxieties escape. Part of the convention of the monologue is that Kenneth shifts focus from a scene with his wife Hilary to one with his lover Laura. So the speech has to bridge these two moments and capture the contradiction of two simultaneous relationships. Kenneth has to juggle relationships just as he juggles words. The speech is manic with emotion, panic and guilt.

Women Laughing
Michael Wall

Act 1. A suburban garden in Ealing, West London.

Tony Catchpole (30) is 'withdrawn . . . a person of low spirits'. He and his wife Maddy are visiting Colin and his wife Stephanie. He has been seeing a psychiatrist and has started group therapy twice a week. Tony and Colin are sitting in the garden, drinking and eating crêpes, making barbed small talk. But every so often from inside the house they hear their wives laughing. Their own conversation is awkward and humdrum – their topics include wine, business and foreigners. They are playing a status game, warily stalking each other. They begin to wonder just what their wives are laughing at. The laughter irritates and intrigues them. In this speech Tony, who has had two gin and tonics and a couple of beers, gets a bit more edgily expansive.

TONY (*eating*). Cheers. Garden's looking very nice.
[COLIN. Hm?]
The garden. I say the garden's looking very nice, the garden.
[COLIN. Oh yeah. It has its moments, doesn't it.]
Maddy does our garden really. Gives her something to do, you know. I think she gets a bit cheesed-off sat at home all day so it provides a pleasant diversion. I mean kids are all right but you have to talk such rubbish to them, don't you? You have to wait sixteen years before you can converse with them and even then its 'Eh mum, I got pimples!' or '*Why* can't I stay out tonight?' We went over to that garden centre in Alexandra Palace and bought some trellises – they were £20 cheaper than exactly the same ones at that place in Highgate. Ridiculous, isn't it? Anyway, we got some Russian vine and – I don't know what else really – clematis,

123

could it be? – anyway we bought all these rambling plants and we're growing them up the trellises.

[COLIN. Oh they're all daffodils to me old chap, except roses.]

Well, we decided it was time we had a little bit more privacy, you know, from over the back. You're all right here; they can't see over, but you know, at our place – they can see right over, see everything you're doing, sort of thing. It does make you sort of tense sometimes, you know? I mean in your own garden. Plus they've got a rather unruly dog which keeps jumping over the wall, so we put up the trellis and it can't do it now. And we can grow stuff on it – quite nice, some of that vine, you know, and it doesn't half grow fast. Sort of creeper stuff it is really. And you can train it; it isn't just random. It's already knee-height and we only bought it last Sunday. No, it was Saturday 'cos we had to go over to Maddy's mum on the Sunday, that's it. Shall I eat this other one as well, only it's a shame to let them go cold.

[COLIN. Please do, Tony.]

All right, you talked me into it. (*Eats.*) Mm, this one appears to have leek in it. I never thought I liked leek, but this is quite nice. You're doing it again.

[COLIN. What?]

You're looking at me like Boris Karloff again.

COMMENTARY: Tony is a man on the edge of a major breakdown. He takes the conversation in what sounds like a neutral direction. But in the midst of talking about his garden we hear how alienated he is from his family. His garden also sounds like a prison with climbing plants shielding him from the outside world. His tension about the neighbours and life in general, manifests itself in his tangled and twisted thoughts. Later in this scene Tony confesses that he has often felt the urge to kill his wife, in fact 'I had it earlier on actually. When I heard you laughing in there. I wanted to go in

124

there and – I wanted to end that tinkling, chiming laugh, just put an end to it.' At the end of this speech he comes to an abrupt stop, signalling the paranoia and anxiety that Tony suffers. The actor should remember that the women laughing inside the house unsettle him deeply.

Your Home in the West
Rod Wooden

Act 2. The living room of a first floor council flat in the West End
of Newcastle upon Tyne. A Friday afternoon in late November
1987.

*Micky Robson (mid-30s) is divorced from his former wife Jean. He is a
foul-mouthed, violent womanizer. He met Jean when they were both
teenagers 'just hanging about the streets'. The two of them set up as a
team together working the Elswick Road; she would proposition men
and then he would rob them. He had a tough childhood; when his father
abandoned the family he was put into care and soon drifted into a life of
petty crime, leading to spells in borstal. He still 'runs round' after girls
and he is now 'stopping' with a seventeen-year-old. Tattooed on his
knuckles are the words 'LET'S FUCK'. When they divorced, Jean got
custody of their children, fifteen-year-old Sharon and seven-year-old
Michael who is a tearaway always truanting from school. Micky dotes
on Michael and spoils him, although Jean thinks he is doing this as a
way of getting back at her. He also has a soft spot for his elderly and
unwell mother and his 'backward' brother, Maurice. When Michael
does another bunk from school his teacher, Jill, comes to visit Jean at
home. Micky, who has no time for social workers or any do-gooders,
drops Michael home and turns on Jill in this speech.*

MICKY (*coming back downstage*). Ever walked round here
in daylight? Ever got out of your little car and walked around
here?
[JILL. I'm a teacher, we don't . . .
MICKY (*interrupting*). Thought not.
Pause MICKY looks out over the audience.
JILL. I'm a *teacher*, we don't . . .
MICKY (*interrupting*).] So you've never noticed all the
126

houses boarded up. How everything's grey, or brown. No curtains at the windows. Just faces, watching you. And nobody walking about. Just a few kids and dogs, and that's it. Or maybe there's a gang of lads trying to tidy up the place with a bloke watching them, kids doing a piddly-shit job for piddly-shit money. Never noticed how they always leave someone in the house, 'cos they're shit scared some fucker's going to break in and pinch whatever it is they haven't got. How they never open the door if they don't know who you are. Just want to sit like slugs waiting for their giros to come. Like they're not alive. Dead. (*Pause.*)

[JILL (*quietly*). I didn't kill them, Mr Robson.]

And then you come on the scene. Or someone like you. From Gosforth. From Jesmond. From some other fucking planet. Like vultures flying over the desert. And you see all this . . . shit. Now what? Don't want to get your hands messed up. I mean, you've got to go back to that nice little house in Gosforth, haven't you? So you put on your rubber gloves and you just . . . (*Gesture.*) . . . rearrange it. You move this pile of shit to over there. Tidy it up a bit. Sort out the dead from the nearly dead. Just like vultures. Take this kid into care cos he's not going to school, get this wife another three quid on her giro. And they just stand there, gobstruck. Like . . . uhhhh. While you just faff about, like a fart in a thunderstorm. Writing everything down. Wanting to know the ins and outs of a duck's arse hole. And they tell you . . . uhhhh. (*He turns to face them.*) And then you fly back up to the sky. Leaving all the shit behind you. Only now it's in smaller piles.

COMMENTARY: Micky is a menace. He's full of sarcasm and virulent anger. He's also an expert at inflicting guilt. Here he has a new victim in Jill. What Micky does so well is sketch a bleak, dehumanized portrait of a Newcastle housing estate. It seems like a carcass waiting to be picked clean. This is a potent portrait of a world that breeds no-hopers; a refuse heap that is disintegrating into a sewer. The anger builds and builds and must be sustained because Micky only explodes fully at the end of the play.

Play Sources

Angels in America by Tony Kushner (Nick Hern Books)

Assassins by Stephen Sondheim and John Weidman (TCG/Nick Hern Books)

Babies by Jonathan Harvey (Methuen)

Belfry by Billy Roche in *The Wexford Trilogy* (Nick Hern Books)

Berlin Bertie by Howard Brenton (Nick Hern Books)

Boy with Beer by Paul Boakye in *Black Plays: Three* (Methuen)

Boys' Life by Howard Korder (Dramatists Play Service)

Burn This by Lanford Wilson (Warner Chappell)

Cigarettes and Chocolate by Anthony Minghella in *Interior: Room Exterior: City* (Methuen)

Dancing Attendance by Lucy Gannon (Warner Chappell)

Death and the Maiden by Ariel Dorfman (Nick Hern Books)

Dog by Steven Berkoff in *Steven Berkoff The Collected Plays: Volume II* (Faber)

Etta Jenks by Marlane Meyer (Methuen)

The Fastest Clock in the Universe by Philip Ridley (Methuen)

Frankie and Johnny in the Clair de Lune by Terrence McNally (Warner Chappell)

The Gigli Concert by Tom Murphy in *Murphy Plays: Three* (Methuen)

Hard Feelings by Doug Lucie in *Fashion, Progress, Hard Feelings & Doing the Business* (Methuen)

Imagine Drowning by Terry Johnson (Methuen)

La Bête by David Hirson (Dramatists Play Service)

The Last Yankee by Arthur Miller (Methuen)

Laughing Wild by Christopher Durang (Samuel French)

Molly Sweeney by Brian Friel (Penguin)

Moonlight by Harold Pinter (Faber)

The Normal Heart by Larry Kramer (Methuen)

Oleanna by David Mamet (Methuen)

The Pitchfork Disney by Philip Ridley (Methuen)

Playing by the Rules by Rod Dungate in *Gay Plays: Five* (Methuen)

Progress by Doug Lucie *Fashion, Progress, Hard Feelings & Doing the Business* (Methuen)

Search and Destroy by Howard Korder (Dramatists Play Service)

Serious Money by Caryl Churchill (Methuen)

Six Degrees of Separation by John Guare (Methuen)

Someone Who'll Watch Over Me by Frank McGuinness (Faber)

Speed-the-Plow by David Mamet (Methen)

States of Shock by Sam Shepard (Methuen)

Talking Heads by Alan Bennett (BBC Books)

Three Hotels by Jon Robin Baitz (Samuel French)

To by Jim Cartwright (Methuen)

Two Shakespearean Actors by Richard Nelson (Faber)

A Wholly Healthy Glasgow by Iain Heggie (Methuen)

The Woman Who Cooked her Husband by Debbie Isitt (Warner Chappell)

Women Laughing by Michael Wall (Micheline Steinberg, Playwrights' Agent, 110 Frognal, London NW3 6XU)

Your Home in the West by Rod Wooden (Methuen)

Acknowledgements

The editors and publishers gratefully acknowledge permission to reproduce copyright material in this book:

Jon Robin Baitz: *Three Hotels*. Copyright © 1992, 1993 by Available Light Productions, Inc. Reprinted by permission of the author's agent, William Morris Agency, 1350 Avenue of the Americas, New York, NY 10019, USA. Alan Bennett: from *Talking Heads*. Copyright © 1988 by Forelake Ltd. Reprinted by permission of BBC Books. Steven Berkoff: from *Dog*. Copyright © 1994 by Steven Berkoff. Reprinted by permission of Faber and Faber Ltd. Paul Boakye: from *Boy with Beer*. Copyright © 1992 by Paul Boakye. Reprinted by permission of Methuen London. Howard Brenton: from *Berlin Bertie*. Copyright © 1992 by Howard Brenton. Reprinted by permission of Nick Hern Books. Jim Cartwright: from *To*. Copyright © 1991 by Jim Cartwright. Reprinted by permission of Methuen London. Caryl Churchill: from *Serious Money*. Copyright © 1987 by Caryl Churchill. Reprinted by permission of Methuen London. Ariel Dorfman: from *Death and the Maiden*. Copyright © 1990 by Ariel Dorfman. Reprinted by permission of Nick Hern Books. Rod Dungate: from *Playing by the Rules*. Copyright © 1994 by Rod Dungate. Reprinted by permission of Methuen London. Christopher Durang: from *Laughing Wild*. Copyright © 1988 by Christopher Durang. Reprinted by permission of the author's agent Helen Merrill, 435 West 23 Street #1A, New York, NY 10011, USA. Brian Friel: from *Molly Sweeney*. Copyright © 1994 by Brian Friel. Reprinted by permission of Penguin Books Limited. Lucy Gannon: from *Dancing Attendance*. Copyright © 1990 by Lucy Gannon. Reprinted by permission of Warner Chappell Ltd. John Guare: from *Six Degrees of Separation*. Copyright © 1992 by John Guare. Reprinted by permission of Methuen London. Jonathan Harvey: from *Babies*. Copyright © 1994 by Jonathan Harvey.

131

132

133

Methuen Audition Books and Monologues

Annika Bluhm (ed)	**The Methuen Audition Book for Men**
	The Methuen Audition Book for Women
Michael Earley and Philippa Keil (eds)	**The Classical Monologue for Men**
	The Classical Monologue for Women
	The Contemporary Monologue – Men
	The Contemporary Monologue – Women
	The Modern Monologue – Men
	The Modern Monologue – Women
Anne Harvey (ed)	**The Methuen Audition Book for Young Actors**
	The Methuen Duologue Book for Young Actors

Methuen Modern Plays

include work by

Jean Anouilh
John Arden
Margaretta D'Arcy
Peter Barnes
Brendan Behan
Edward Bond
Bertolt Brecht
Howard Brenton
Simon Burke
Jim Cartwright
Caryl Churchill
Noël Coward
Sarah Daniels
Nick Dear
Shelagh Delaney
David Edgar
Dario Fo
Michael Frayn
John Guare
Peter Handke
Jonathan Harvey
Declan Hughes
Terry Johnson

Barrie Keeffe
Stephen Lowe
Doug Lucie
John McGrath
David Mamet
Arthur Miller
Mtwa, Ngema & Simon
Tom Murphy
Peter Nichols
Joe Orton
Louise Page
Luigi Pirandello
Stephen Poliakoff
Franca Rame
David Rudkin
Willy Russell
Jean-Paul Sartre
Sam Shepard
Wole Soyinka
Theatre Workshop
Sue Townsend
Timberlake Wertenbaker
Victoria Wood

Methuen New Theatrescripts

include work by

April de Angelis
Iraj Jannatie Ataie
Harwant Bains
Sebastian Barry
Simone de Beauvoir/
  Diana Quick
Paul Boakye
Richard Cameron
Fred D'Aguiar
Rod Dungate
Marieluise Fleisser/
  Tinch Minter
Nikolai Gogol/Adrian Mitchell
Bonnie Greer
Noël Greig
Jonathan Harvey
Robert Holman
Kevin Hood
Karen Hope
Declan Hughes
Tunde Ikoli

Elfriede Jelinek/Tinch Minter
Judith Johnson
Manfred Karge/Tinch Minter &
  Anthony Vivis
Barrie Keeffe
Thomas Kilroy
Maureen Lawrence
Claire Luckham
Anthony Minghella
Phyllis Nagy
Winsome Pinnock
Joe Pintauro
Philip Ridley
Rob Ritchie
Diane Samuels
David Spencer
Edward Thomas
Michael Wilcox
Nicholas Wright
Rod Wooden
Sheila Yeger